Contents

iii

③ Use of ICT in the banking and finance sector 84

④ Use of ICT to aid travel 104

⑤ Use of ICT in retailing 120

⑥ Designing information systems 140

GCSE
information and communication technology

FOR OCR SPECIFICATION B

ENDORSED BY OCR

Steve Cushing

Heinemann Educational Publishers,
Halley Court, Jordan Hill, Oxford OX2 8EJ
A division of Reed Educational & Professional Publishing Ltd

Heinemann is a registered trademark of Reed Educational & Professional
Publishing Limited

OXFORD MELBOURNE AUCKLAND JOHANNESBURG BLANTYRE
GABORONE IBADAN PORTSMOUTH NH (USA) CHICAGO

© Steve Cushing 2001

First published 2001
2005 2004 2003 2002
10 9 8 7 6 5 4 3 2

A catalogue record for this book is available from the British Library on request.

ISBN 0 435 45496 X

All rights reserved.

Apart from any fair dealing for the purposes of research or private study, or
criticism or review as permitted under the terms of the UK Copyright, Designs
and Patents Act, 1988, this publication may not be reproduced, stored or
transmitted, in any form or by any means, without the prior permission in
writing of the publishers, or in the case of reprographic reproduction only in
accordance with the terms of the licences issued by the Copyright Licensing
Agency in the UK, or in accordance with the terms of licenses issued by the
appropriate Reproduction Rights Organization outside the UK. Enquiries
concerning reproduction outside the terms stated here should be sent to the
publishers at the United Kingdom address printed on this page.

Designed and typeset by Artistix, Thame, Oxon

Printed and bound in Spain by Edelvives

Tel: 01865 888058 www.heinemann.co.uk

Introduction

The world is becoming increasingly dominated by the use of information and communication technology (ICT) systems. These influence every aspect of our lives. Today, new and exciting career opportunities are available to those with the knowledge and skills to use information and communication technology creatively, with whole industries emerging around the ICT revolution.

Today's citizens – and that means you – need to be equipped with knowledge and skills to enable them to participate in a technological society. They need technological and information handling skills that include the ability to gather, process and manipulate data. These skills are now as essential as those of traditional numeracy and literacy. This book explores these changes and will help to prepare you for the world of work. It looks at new technology used today and attempts to take a glimpse into the future.

The increase in the use of new technology has been brought about as much by the convergence, or coming together, of computing and telecommunications as it has by the growth in the use of microprocessors. All of the applications outlined in the book rely upon an ability to transfer data from one place to another.

Few aspects of our society have not been influenced by the ICT revolution. ICT has radically changed the way we work. For example, traditional jobs, such as those in the banking and finance industry, are disappearing while new areas of economic activity, such as e-commerce, are growing rapidly.

The citizen of tomorrow needs to be computer literate as the use of communication networks becomes common and information and communication technologies provide new opportunities for working, learning and living.

Our age is marked by constant and rapid change. In the lifetime of this book, technology will continue to make advances and much of what is now considered state of the art will become obsolete. As well as the rapid development of new technologies that gather, organise and share information, familiar technologies like telephone, television, and computers are evolving and converging.

This book aims to prepare you for this changing society and to help you meet the requirements of the National Curriculum Key Stage 4 Programmes of Study and OCR syllabus (B) ICT GCSE.

The challenge is to develop an understanding of the essentials of information technology and the tools required for preparing and participating in an information-based society. All of us need to have a firm grounding in ICT for our careers, for lifelong learning and for recreation.

To be responsible members of society, we must all be aware of the ever-growing impact of ICT. We need to think carefully about the role of ICT and to consider its positive and negative effects.

Acknowledgements

The author wishes to thank Barbara Yeomans, who conducted a large amount of research and contributed to the text of the book. Without her assistance, the book would not have been possible.

The author and publishers would like to thank the following individuals and organizations for permission to reproduce photographs and other copyright material:

Action plc – page 123
Adobe Systems – pages 67, 68
Alvey and Towers – page 110
Corbis/Bettmann – page 3
Corbis/Christopher Cormack – page 53 (top)
Corbis/Robert Maass – page 44
Corbis/Bob Rowan; Progressive Image – page 65
Corbis/Bill Varie – page 98
Steve Cushing/The Learning Shop – page 72 (right)
Steve Cushing, with kind permission of Northampton Theatres – pages 46, 48, 51
Haddon Davies – page 85
Ecoscene/Tony Page – page 117
Ecoscene/Rod Smith – page 112
FPG International – page 4
FTMarketwatch.com – page 100
Chris Honeywell – page 23 (left)
Imagebank/Peter Pacifica – page 53 (bottom)
Kodak – page 64
Londonstills.com – page 104
Macromedia – page 72 (left)
Microsoft – pages 11, 17, 33, 72, 81, 100, 105, 123

Peter Morris – pages 24, 64 (inset)
Nationwide – page 84
Northampton Theatres – pages 69, 71
OCR – page 21
Photodisc – pages 23 (right), 25
Ryanair – page 105
Safeway – page 125
Science Photo Library/Samuel Ashfield – page 19
Science Photo Library/Alex Bartel – page 140
Science Photo Library/Deep Light Productions – page 20 (left)
Science Photo Library/James King-Holmes – page 113
Science Photo Library/R. Maisonneuve, Publiphoto Diffusion – page 26
Science Photo Library/Jerry Mason – page 89
Science Photo Library/St Bartholomew's Hospital – page 2
Science Photo Library/Weiss, Jerrican – page 116
Stone/Mark Douet – page 20 (right)
Techsoft – page 128
Teletext – page 108
Tesco – pages 131, 135
Zefa – page 111

Cover photographs:
Robbie Jack – bottom left
SPL – bottom right
Tony Stone – top left and right

Every effort has been made to contact copyright holders of material published in this book. We would be glad to hear from unacknowledged sources at the first opportunity.

Using this book

This book has been written to help you understand ICT and its use in the world of work.

It has been divided into five sections. These look at the effects of ICT and how it is used in each of the following areas of work:

- health care services
- entertainment
- banking and finance
- travel
- retailing.

Each section introduces a knowledge of information technology hardware and software that is required for the area of work being covered. To avoid repetition, background information on hardware and software is given only once – the first time it appears in each section. In this way, ICT is presented as a tool to make things happen, rather than as an end in itself. For detailed information on hardware and software, you will need to refer to the section where it appears.

Each section contains two different kinds of text:

- black text is used to describe ICT in the context of the various industries covered in each section
- coloured text provides the underpinning knowledge required by the scheme.

As you work through each section, you will be given every opportunity to fulfil the requirements of GCSE and vocational studies. Key words are shown in **bold**.

If you are using this book to carry out a coursework task, you will need to follow the section on Designing information systems as you work through the topic on which you are basing your coursework.

The book contains a large number of activities for you to choose from, or you can devise your own activity.

If you are exploring a topic to prepare notes for use in a context-driven examination, remember that you will have very little time when you are taking the examination to read any notes that you may have been allowed to take into the examination room. For this reason, your notes should be brief, using bullet points and sketches wherever possible.

There are help sheets in the first two sections of the book. These briefly outline all you need to know about certain topics.

Please note that the examples of websites suggested in this book were up to date at the time of writing. It is essential for tutors to preview each site before using it to ensure that the URL is still accurate and the content is appropriate. We suggest that tutors bookmark useful sites and consider enabling students to access them through the school or college intranet.

Use of ICT in the health care services

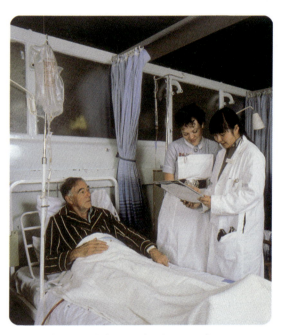

A consultant and doctor check manual paper patient records

Activity:

Design an electronic patient record card. Your card will need to contain details of the patient, including name, sex, age, address, name of GP, next of kin and medical history. The information should be organised in a way that enables it to be entered into a database.

Before the introduction of information and communication technology (ICT), the health service, like most other organisations, used a paper-based system for storing information.

When patients registered with a doctor (or General Practitioner – GP), all of their personal details were recorded, usually on the front of a folder, in which their medical life history could be kept.

When patients changed GP, their medical files had to be transferred by post or via the patients themselves. Each time a patient was seen by the GP, he or she would handwrite notes into the patient's record.

As an example of the problems that could arise with a traditional paper-based system, let's follow an imaginary patient, John:

- During the night, John is ill.

- The doctor on call, who is not his regular doctor, visits him at home.

- John's record card is collected from the GP's surgery and, following his visit to John, the doctor on call leaves John's records on the back seat of his car while he visits other patients.

- John feels much worse and is rushed into hospital by ambulance.

- He is treated in the ambulance itself by a paramedic. The paramedic cannot get access to John's medical notes.

- On arrival at hospital, John is booked first into accident and emergency and then into an emergency ward.

- He undergoes an operation and is then transferred to a recovery ward.

- The hospital receptionist, and numerous doctors and nurses are involved in his care. Once John's medical records have been retrieved from the first doctor on call, each of these people must remember what happened and record it in the patient's notes.

- Until the records have been found, none of the medical specialists can be sure of the details of John's past medical history, nor whether he is currently taking any medicines, or is allergic to any medicines or treatments. They also cannot tell whether there is any family history of the illness that he has.

If John had been referred to the hospital by his GP using the traditional system, a long process would have followed, involving a letter being sent from John's GP to the hospital. A hospital employee would have opened the letter and made a decision about the urgency of John's condition. A letter would then have been sent to John's GP to arrange appointment times.

Activity:

Design a hospital or GP's appointment system based upon a computer database.

Captured by the system

Before **data**, or information, can be used in an **information system** it needs to be entered into the system. The most common way of entering data is through a computer keyboard.

There are several different types of keyboard. The **standard keyboard** and **concept keyboard** are the most common. In a medical environment, it is important to keep everything, including the keyboard, clean and germ free.

Standard keyboard

Keyboards are very reliable as a means of **data input**, both for alphabet characters and numerals, but not all users are able to type either quickly or accurately. Some people may be unable to use keyboards, for example if they suffer paralysis affecting their arms and hands or they are wearing gloves, as a surgeon might do. Specialised keyboards are available for use by disabled people, or for special applications.

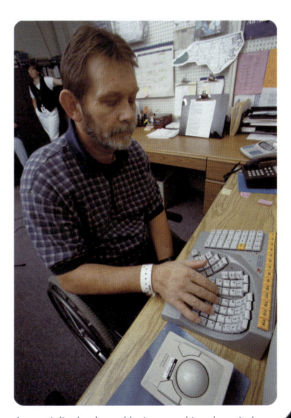

A specialist keyboard being used in a hospital environment

3

Use of ICT in the health care services

Concept keyboard

A nurse or doctor may not need a full keyboard. You will need to think about the type of data being entered and the environment in which data entry takes place. For example, while a GP's surgery will be clean and dry, an operating theatre will be clean but may contain fluids. The surgeon is likely to be wearing gloves. Wherever there are fluids, dust, or you want to restrict or simplify data entry, a concept keyboard can be used.

A concept keyboard is a flat-bed of contact **switches** covered by a flexible membrane. It can be used in some health care situations. System and software designers can allocate one or more switches to respond in different ways.

Often an **overlay** is placed over the keyboard with pictures or symbols.

Concept keyboards are popular anywhere that liquid may be spilt. They can be wiped clean. They are also often found in restaurants, supermarkets, bars and cinemas.

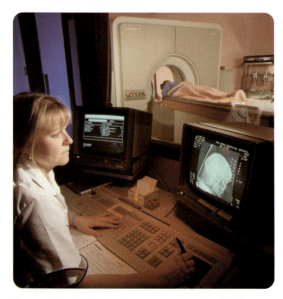

A specialist keyboard used to control a CAT scan machine in a hospital

They are quick and easy to use as they utilise **point and touch methods** of data entry.

Where data or machinery has to be manipulated and managed easily, accurately and quickly, concept or specialist keyboards are often used. Specialist keyboards are similar to concept keyboards but rather than using an overlay the keyboard itself is built to perform a particular task such as controlling a CAT scan machine in a hospital.

Activity:

Design a concept keyboard overlay for use in a hospital environment.

Activity:

Explore a range of data input methods suitable for a medical environment.

Managing the data

Managing data and information is the key to maintaining accurate medical records. A database would normally be used to **sort**, **store**, **search** and **retrieve** information about the patient.

It is important to be clear about the difference between data and information.

- **Data** is the raw values that are entered into, stored and processed by information systems. Examples would be the recordings of a patient's temperature, or heartbeat when the patient is being monitored continuously. Data can be stored in a number of ways.

- **Information** is produced as output and feedback, with a context that gives it meaning. An example of this would be the report that is produced as a result of monitoring a patient's temperature or heartbeat, showing the patient's state of health.

Both data and information are useful in a health care setting. Hospitals and GPs' surgeries will hold data on their ICT systems. It is information about allergies, medical treatment and next of kin that hospital staff will need in order to treat patients safely.

The key to any medical system is an accurate and effective database.

Many hospitals' and GPs' systems are developed specifically for the health care environment using **tailor-made software**. You can develop your own systems using a **general purpose** database package. General purpose packages are useful because their documentation (manuals, tutorials, etc.) are usually excellent, programs are well tested and the packages are inexpensive.

Hospitals and GPs' surgeries will not want to spend more money than is necessary, as anything they buy will take money away from other forms of patient care.

The types of software you might use include: Microsoft Access, PinPoint, dBase.

Designing and constructing databases

Before you design a database system, you need to be clear about what information is required and how it should be structured. The structure of a database is very important. The best starting point for a medical database is the existing hospital system.

Files, records and fields

Databases are constructed using **files**, **records** and **fields**.

A hospital system will have a number of different files. One file will contain all of the patients' details; another the nurses' and doctors' details. There may be a file of medicines and medical equipment.

A file might contain all of the dietary requirements of medical conditions.

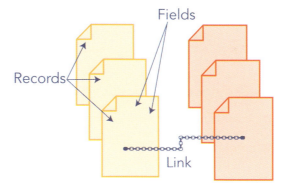

Medical files

In addition to medical files, a large hospital will need a file to enable the hospital's caterers to cope with a wide range of conflicting needs. The right diet is just as important to a healthy recovery as the right medicines and treatment. The caterers will have a limited amount of money to spend, patients will want to be able to select from a range of foods, but many of the foods produced have to be tailored for individual special diets needed for different medical conditions.

Activity:

Design a system for food ordering and production in a hospital environment.

Each file will consist of a series of records. Each record might represent a single patient, or a medicine. Each of these records is made up of a number of pieces of information, called fields.

In the case of a patient, each record will contain the following fields: the patient's name, sex, age, doctor, medical condition and medical history.

Activity:

Design a system for costing food use in a hospital environment.

There are two main types of database:

- a **flat-file** database
- a **relational** database.

Flat-file databases

In a flat-file database all the data is stored in a single file, and the sorting, searching and printing of reports is all done in this single file.

This makes flat-file databases:

- easy to use
- suitable for small amounts of data.

But they are probably not suitable for a health care setting, where large quantities of data need to be stored.

Relational databases

In relational databases, the tables, or files, of data exist independently from the programs that may use them. Relational databases use **database management systems (DBMS)** to link independent files together.

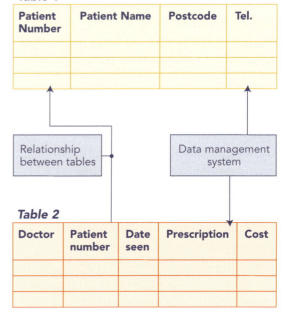

Table 1

Patient Number	Patient Name	Postcode	Tel.

Relationship between tables	Data management system

Table 2

Doctor	Patient number	Date seen	Prescription	Cost

A database management system

A hospital would use a relational database. Sometimes different users, such as doctors, nurses and patients, will have access to data stored in different files. However, not all users will be given permission to look at all the data.

When designing a relational database such as that used in a hospital, the first thing to decide is which fields you will need and what order of importance they should be in.

It is usual to select one field as a **key field**. A key field represents a unique item of information in each person's record.

An individual record can be located in the file by using its unique key field. The unique key field is usually used in a relational database to link files. Names are not normally used as key fields since more than one patient could have the same name. Other patients might not want to be known by their real names.

Each field should be given a suitable field name. Data can take two forms.

It can be in the form of numbers, called **numeric data** such as patient temperature, date of birth, age, and telephone numbers; or text, referred to as **character data** such as names and addresses. Sometimes data will contain both numbers and text, in which case it is called **alphanumeric**, for example post codes. Fields can also be **date fields** or **logical true/false fields**. For example, does the patient have an allergy to penicillin? Yes/No = Y/N. The date and even the time when medicine is administered could be very important to doctors using a medical database.

True/false fields can hold only a single character or numeral. Date fields can hold only a date. The other fields can vary in length. When you are designing a database, you will need to decide on a maximum field length. This is usually achieved by examining a sample of the data you intend to enter into each field.

Ensuring data is accurate

When designing a hospital database, it is essential to ensure that data typed in is accurate. This is achieved by **verification** and **validation** checking.

Verification checks

A verification check makes sure that data that has been entered, or copied from another source, has been transferred correctly. There are various ways of carrying out verification checks.

Sometimes, where data is to be entered via a keyboard, two operators may be asked to enter the same data. The two versions can then be compared and, if they match, the data is stored. If not, the source document is looked at to see where mistakes have been made. Any mistakes can then be corrected and stored. This type of verification checking is time consuming because two people are required to do one job.

One simple way of trying to verify input data is to display it on the screen and ask the operator who has entered it to read it through and indicate if it is correct. Unfortunately, operators often do not see their own mistakes, or do not believe that they have made any mistakes and therefore do not even read through the data before confirming it is correct.

A **parity check** makes use of the **binary code** understood by the computer to try to make sure that data is not **corrupted** during transfer. When groups of **bits** (1s and 0s) are being transferred, an extra bit is added so that the total number of 1s is always odd (or, alternatively, always even). This is called the parity of the data. One incorrectly transmitted bit will change the parity, making it possible to detect the error. However, if an even number of incorrect bits has been transmitted, the parity is not changed. Even though not all errors are detected, the user is warned by those that are indicated and can check the data more thoroughly to locate others.

Activity:

Design a system of verification or parity checking for a hospital database.

Validation checks

Validation checking is carried out by the software to make sure that data is sensible and will not cause problems when it is processed.

Various types of validation check detect different types of error. Type checks make sure that numeric data does not accidentally contain letters. For example, an accidental letter 'O' in place of a zero would be noticed.

A **range check** is used to make sure that data is inside a fixed set of values. For example, date of birth might have to be between 1900 and present date. A range check can be used with letters as well as numbers. A set range of letters can be specified. For example, authors of books on one shelf rack in a medical library might have names beginning with any letter from N to S.

A **presence check** makes sure that a value has actually been entered in a particular field. This type of check is used where certain vital data must be entered. An example would be a patient's blood group where a hospital has to give a blood transfusion.

Patient records must be accurate and up to date. Any error could cost a patient his or her life.

Check digits

Check digits are used widely to validate numeric data, especially where numbers with many digits are being entered.

The check digit is a single digit number calculated from all the rest of the digits in a data item and then attached to the end of the data when it is stored. Check digits are present in **barcode** numbers and are also used in account numbers.

There is a check digit in the ISBN on a book. It can be used to detect **transposition errors** – when two digits are entered the wrong way round – and to detect changes or losses of digits in numbers. When an operator inputs the number, the check digit is recalculated and the two versions are compared. If they match, the data is correct and can be saved. If they do not match, there is a mistake and the number has to be re-input.

Help sheet 1: databases

The content (1) and structure (2) phase is where the scope of the project is decided and plans are made accordingly.

1 Decide on content (what needs to be stored)

- What is the function and purpose of the database?
- What does the database replace?
- What and how much data do you want to store?
- Nature and range of any searches that will be required.
- What types of reports are needed?
- Identify audience – who will use your system?
- Identify context – where and how will your system be viewed?
- List key points.

2 Structure of database

- Look at other examples.
- Identify the *scope* of the project.
- Files, fields and types of data.
- Key fields and links.
- Size and field lengths.
- Verification and validation checking.
- User interface and screen layout – produce flowcharts of possible sequences.
- Navigation interface – buttons, options and icons.
- Who needs to access the data? Access and passwords.
- Backing up the data.

3 Choose hardware and software

Only prototypes of the product are produced in this phase. Once you create anything that will be used in the final product, you have moved into the production phase.

- Select possible hardware platform/software packages for delivery.
- Define user environment/hardware limitations.
- Determine output requirements (screen, web, monitor).

4 Production

You should start to make your system only once you have decided the exact content and goals of the project.

- Create user interface:
  - input and output
  - usability test (your response).
- Assemble all elements into data structure.
- Create/import data:
  - validate and verify.
- Create lookup tables.
- Create reports.

5 Evaluation (Does it work?)

- Usability test (user response):
  - searches, data entry and stability.
- 'Debug' session.
- Evaluate content or structure that requires modification.
- Revise (at whatever level necessary).
- Produce user documentation.

Quality of data – accuracy and truth

It is important to remember that although verification checks will attempt to ensure that data is copied correctly, and validation checks will pinpoint data that has numerical or character errors, there is no way of making sure that the data entered into a computer system is either accurate or true.

Nobody has yet written software that can act as a lie detector. It is up to the user to make sure that data entered is accurate, otherwise **outputs** from the system will be wrong. Remember, if you put rubbish in, you will get rubbish out.

Patient records need to be as truthful as possible, but much of the data will rely upon information that patients themselves supply. They may not want to tell the truth, particularly if previous illnesses have been of an embarrassing nature.

The question of truth is a difficult one, particularly in relation to the **Internet**. Web pages are innocently used by thousands of people as **electronic reference books**, but there is no check on the quality of information displayed on them. The user can only hope that, if the site is provided by a reputable organisation, the information offered can be believed.

On a medical database, it may be important to record where the data has come from. This could include which doctor or nurse entered the data, and might even contain a true/false field where the doctor or nurse can indicate whether he or she believes the patient is telling the truth.

Adding, deleting and updating records

Once the database structure is complete, data can be input in the form of records. Having tried to ensure data accuracy, it is essential to protect the database from any future corruption or damage. In a health care setting, one way to protect a database is to ensure that only authorised people can add or amend records.

Activity:

Design a security system for a hospital database.

Using the database

You will need to consider the **interface** between the database and **end user**. When you design the way data is shown on the screen, you should have the skills and requirements of the end user in mind – the system will probably be used by non-specialists, so it will need to be clear and simple to use.

To search for (extract) information from a database, the user carries out a query, or interrogation. For example, you might search to find all patients over a certain age, or with a certain medical condition. The larger the database, the more important it is to draw up effective search conditions. The terms **AND**, **OR** and **NOT** are used to define precisely what is being searched for:

- AND is used to include two or more criteria (items) in a search.

- OR is used to indicate that either one or another criterion is acceptable.

- NOT is used to restrict a search so that it does not include the criterion that follows NOT.

Sorting information

A user may wish to sort information from a database. For example, you may want an alphabetical list of patient surnames. This is achieved by using a **sort** command.

The sort command can usually be used on only one field at a time, and when it is used, a new file is produced that has the same contents as the original file, but in a different order. This means that although the ability to sort data is very useful and quick, performing several sorts on a large database could mean that you would run out of disk space because of the new files created.

A database program allows the user, in our example, the hospital, health centre or GP, to handle files, keep records in an organised way and retrieve information from these records. You could do these via the screen or printer.

Other types of files such as X-rays and ultrasound scan pictures may need to be linked to a medical database.

Activity:

Design a database system that can easily link to picture files such as X-rays.

The doctor will use the database to combine results into a report.

Typical medical applications of databases include creating and maintaining personal lists such as:

- details of patients' names, addresses and medical or dental records
- patient medical history
- visits to see the GP
- prescriptions issued
- allergies
- lists of suppliers to the hospital or dispensary (where prescriptions are made up for patients).

Data protection

Data about our medical history is private and confidential. To stop it falling into the wrong hands we are protected by the Data Protection Act (1998).

Microsoft Access - [Categories : Table]

File Edit View Insert Format Records Tools Window Help

Category ID	Category Name	Description	Picture
1	Beverages	Soft drinks, coffees, teas, beers and ales	Bitmap image
2	Condiments	Sweet and savoury sauces, relishes, spreads and seasonings	Bitmap image
3	Confections	Desserts, candies, and sweet breads	Bitmap image
4	Dairy Products	Cheeses	Bitmap image
5	Grains/Cereals	Breads, crackers, pasta, and cereal	Bitmap image
6	Meat/Poultry	Prepared meats	Bitmap image
7	Produce	Dried fruit and bean curd	Bitmap image
8	Seafood	Seaweed and fish	Bitmap image
(AutoNumber)			

A database package

Data Protection Act (1998)

The 1998 Data Protection Act relates to any personal data that may be stored. Personal data is defined in the Act as being data relating to living individuals who can be identified from that data. This means that general data collected from **point of sale** terminals and **websites** does not come under the Act but as soon as it is linked to a living individual, it must comply with the Act.

The requirements of the 1998 Act also cover many categories of manually held data, not just data held in electronic format. It includes a section specifically aimed at Internet use of data.

These are some of the types of data that companies need to register under the Act:

- Public and internal directories (students, customers, staff, friends, etc.) – includes names, e-mail addresses, postal addresses, phone numbers and any other contact information such as house or business location, purchasing preferences and habits.

- Staff and customer biographical information pages – includes qualifications, career history, photographs, publications, personal information, etc.

- Web pages linking to management databases – includes a number of categories including some very sensitive data.

- Mandatory or voluntary online forms (registration forms, information requests, etc.) – includes names, e-mail addresses, postal addresses, phone numbers and other contact information.

- Online research surveys – includes data that identifies any individual response to a survey.

- E-mail list subscriptions ('Subscribe to receive regular news', etc.) – names, e-mail addresses and possibly other information.

There are other ways that companies could be caught out by the Act. These might include the use of server-based cookie file systems, scripts that enable web pages to be personalised, or possibly scripts that capture environment variables such as REMOTE_USER, REMOTE_IDENT and HTTP_FROM or otherwise move into a user's system to retrieve data.

If companies collect any of the data outlined above they must appoint a data controller and register with the **Information Commissioner**.

Before processing personal data, data controllers are required to notify the Information Commissioner of:

- their name and address

- the data to be processed

- the category or categories of data subject to which they relate

- the purposes for which the data will be processed.

Before being registered, companies are checked to ensure the security of personal data held. The Act places a legal obligation on data controllers to follow eight data protection principles (see opposite). They also have to register who the data will be accessed by and provide a list of countries outside the European Economic Area (EEA) to which data may be transferred. (The EEA includes Austria, Belgium, Denmark, Finland, France, Germany, Greece, Ireland, Italy, Luxembourg, the Netherlands, Portugal, Spain, Sweden, Switzerland and the UK, plus Iceland, Liechtenstein and Norway.) This can cause problems for Internet-based companies, banks, theatres and retailers where activities are not limited to the EEA.

The eight principles

1. Personal data shall be processed fairly and lawfully and, in particular, shall not be processed unless:

    a at least one of the conditions in Schedule 2 of the Act is met, and

    b in the case of sensitive personal data, at least one of the conditions in Schedule 3 is also met.

2. Personal data shall be obtained only for one or more specified and lawful purposes, and shall not be further processed in any manner incompatible with that purpose or those purposes.

3. Personal data shall be adequate, relevant and not excessive in relation to the purpose or purposes for which it is processed.

4. Personal data shall be accurate and, where necessary, kept up to date.

5. Personal data processed for any purpose or purposes shall not be kept for longer than is necessary for that purpose or those purposes.

6. Personal data shall be processed in accordance with the rights of data subjects under the Act.

7. Appropriate technical and organisational measures shall be taken against unauthorised or unlawful processing of personal data and against accidental loss or destruction of, or damage to, personal data.

8. Personal data shall not be transferred to a country or territory outside the European Economic Area unless that country or territory ensures an adequate level of protection for the rights and freedoms of data subjects in relation to the processing of personal data.

The first principle prevents all processing of personal data unless at least one of six conditions are met, the first of which is that the data subject has given his or her consent. Obtaining the data subject's consent is therefore probably going to be the key to ensuring the legality of the processing of personal data on the Internet as it is the easiest way of complying with the Act.

Obtaining consent is also one of the possible cases under which the eighth principle could come into effect as it prevents the transfer of personal data outside the EEA.

The aim of this eighth principle is to ensure that personal data can be transferred freely between EEA member states (to facilitate job applications, free trade, etc.) but also to prevent data from being transferred to a country with a different approach to data privacy.

One such country is the USA, where industry associations administer rules on the protection of data privacy on a self-regulated basis. There is no US law that matches the rigorous principles of European Union (EU) law, and so, in theory, no personal data held in an EU country (even if it relates to a US citizen) can be legally transferred to the USA without the permission of the person concerned, on a case-by-case basis, and only for a specific reason.

This can cause major problems for banks and online retailers as the eighth principle also effectively prevents the publication of personal data on public web pages and Internet access to data as it is not possible to control access from specific countries.

The advice given by the **Data Protection Office** makes it clear that obtaining consent must involve 'active communication between the parties' and that 'data controllers cannot *assume* consent if someone does not respond to a communication'.

Under the 1984 Data Protection Act, the title given to the person overseeing the Register of Data was Data Protection Registrar. When the new Act of 1998 came into force, the Registrar's name was changed to Data Protection Commissioner. In 2001, with the introduction of the Freedom of Information Act, the name changed again to Information Commissioner.

Any forms used for gathering personal data from visitors to a website, or any procedures in place within an organisation to collect personal data for publication on a website must now give an opportunity for the data subjects to give or withhold their consent to the proposed processing or publication of the data.

Paper-based systems

One of the difficulties faced by the health care profession is the wide range of care offered. This care can be provided not only by several GPs within one surgery or health centre, but also by a wide range of other health care professionals. For example, for a single medical treatment,

an emergency doctor could first visit you at home. You might then visit your own GP at his or her own surgery. You might be admitted to hospital. In the hospital, you might be dealt with by doctors, surgeons, anaesthetists, nurses and a range of other health care specialists. On leaving hospital, you might be assigned a health visitor to monitor your progress. All of these health care workers need access to your records.

To enable you to examine such records in more detail, we will start with just one of these stages, the GP's surgery. First, we will examine a paper-based system. This is the type of system that was used before the widespread introduction of electronic ICT systems.

Patients' notes

In a paper-based system, visits to the GP's surgery were relatively simple in that the receptionist would manually find the notes and give them to the doctor. Visits to hospital or other doctors were not so simple, particularly in emergencies, because the patient's notes would not be readily available. In some large hospitals, paper-based patients' notes took up a large amount of space and were often misplaced.

Activity:

Design an ICT system that could track a patient's records or the location of a patient's records.

But it was not just lost notes that caused problems. Even if the notes were available, particularly in emergencies, other health care workers could not always read the handwriting of those who had written the patient's notes. In hospital, a patient could be seen by a large number of different people, who would all be expected to contribute to the notes.

Prescriptions

In a traditional medical practice, prescriptions were written by hand and where patients required more than a standard supply of a prescription, they needed to revisit the surgery for a repeat prescription.

Activity:

Design an automatic prescription application that will enable a patient to type in his or her own details and, after an electronic check, receive a printed prescription.

ICT offers an ideal solution to problems of reading handwriting. **Word processing** software could be used. The types of software you might use include: Microsoft Word, WordPerfect.

Word processing software

Word processing has several advantages over pen and paper, or a typewriter. The main advantage is the ability to change or correct what you have typed. This is of vital importance in a health care setting.

Word processors enable the user to:

- insert text

- delete text
- justify text
- move text around
- alter margin settings
- use tabs
- change fonts and font sizes
- alter line spacing.

A wide range of other specialist options is available. For example, data can be linked to other packages using hyperlinks and pasting links. A medical database could easily be linked to word processing files containing doctors' notes.

Activity:

Design a system that will import data from a database for use in a prescription.

Most modern word processors have spelling and grammar checkers and will also allow you to search for and replace text and even compare two documents to look for differences between them. Where specialist terms are used, such as in a health care setting, a user dictionary of medical words would need to be created.

Activity:

Explore the use of specialist dictionaries and devise a word processing system for doctors to use. Your system must enable doctors to use specialist medical terms.

Integrating word processing packages with other software packages

Modern health centres and hospitals use word processing to produce letters, memos, reports, lists and other text documents. They also use this type of software to produce sets of similar letters, with personalised details, to be sent to patients. This technique is called **mail merge**. A list of letter recipients is compiled, either by the word processor, or by importing data from a database, a standard letter is created, and the personalised data inserted into blanks in each letter.

Activity:

Design a system that uses mail merge to remind patients of a hospital appointment.

Modern word processing packages will also **import** text and images from other programs. Health care staff might want to import data from a medical database into word processed documents.

Once imported, **text** and **graphics** can be amended and the position on the page can be changed. However, desktop publishing packages are designed more with these functions in mind, and therefore offer simpler ways of carrying out these tasks.

Most word processing packages will also allow you to add **tables** and **formulae**. The formulae are similar to those used in a spreadsheet package.

Activity:

Devise a system that can link database, spreadsheet and word processing files.

Saving your work

Saving your work regularly is very important. This can be done using one of two main commands:

- **Save**
- **Save As**.

It is important to note the difference between these two commands:

- The Save command overwrites the existing file.
- The Save As command allows you to save a different version of the file.

Most word processing packages allow you to set up an automatic save function so that your work is saved automatically at set intervals.

Word processing software will allow health care staff to produce text for uses such as letters and reports. It will allow simple entry and editing of text, and correction of errors. A word processor can normally check spelling and grammar, and can offer a thesaurus to increase vocabulary choices. Standard prescription formats could be designed and saved as a template for later use.

Activity:

Design a system for the production of prescriptions.

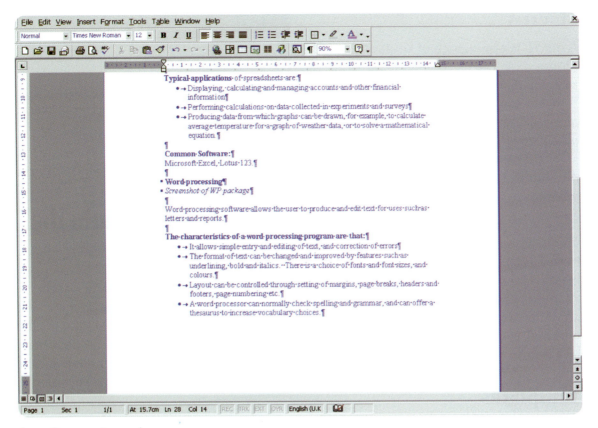

The window shows a word processing application with the following document content:

Typical·applications· of·spreadsheets·are:¶
- →Displaying,·calculating·and·managing·accounts·and·other·financial·information¶
- →Performing·calculations·on·data·collected·in·experiments·and·surveys¶
- →Producing·data·from·which·graphs·can·be·drawn,·for·example,·to·calculate·average·temperature·for·a·graph·of·weather·data,·or·to·solve·a·mathematical·equation.¶

Common·Software:¶
Microsoft·Excel,·Lotus·123.¶

- Word·processing¶
- Screenshot·of·WP·package¶

Word·processing·software·allows·the·user·to·produce·and·edit·text·for·uses·such·as·letters·and·reports.¶

The·characteristics·of·a·word·processing·program·are·that:¶
- →It·allows·simple·entry·and·editing·of·text,·and·correction·of·errors¶
- →The·format·of·text·can·be·changed·and·improved·by·features·such·as·underlining,·bold·and·italics.··There·is·a·choice·of·fonts·and·font·sizes,·and·colours.¶
- →Layout·can·be·controlled·through·setting·of·margins,·page·breaks,·headers·and·footers,·page·numbering·etc.¶
- →A·word·processor·can·normally·check·spelling·and·grammar,·and·can·offer·a·thesaurus·to·increase·vocabulary·choices.¶

A word processing package

Word processing can also allow a user to highlight words in a text that are to be included in an index, and can then create the index. It can find specific words in a text and replace them if required to do so. It provides facilities for printing and addressing sets of printed letters or memos. This could be used to remind a patient about a forthcoming GP or hospital appointment.

Speeding up data entry

All health care staff will be very busy people. They will not want to waste time typing and retyping the same data, such as patient names, addresses and basic details. They will also need a user friendly interface.

To speed up data entry your prescription could include a **barcode**. Although bar-codes are more commonly used in retailing, they could be used to save the pharmacist having to retype patient or medicine details and could help in circumstances where repeat prescriptions are required.

Data entry can be speeded up by using **macros** to personalise the word processor.

Alongside **templates** and **style sheets** it is possible to reduce the time the health care staff have to spend at the **terminal** and free them up for other patient care activities.

Macros

A macro is a sequence of keystrokes, mouse movements or other commands that you can record and then play back. A macro can be played back by pressing a single key, selecting a menu or clicking on an icon. You can modify most software using macros, and make it more productive by producing personal interfaces.

Most word processing programs allow you to assign a macro to a menu item or button bar. Some even provide you with button icons to choose from. For example, you can create a macro to automatically fax a document via the Internet. You can then assign the macro to a button that looks like a fax machine.

Templates

A template can contain text, macros, formatting codes and any other information that you need to create a customised document. Hospitals could have a special template for memos, letters and invoices. Most major word processing programs come with a range of templates already formatted. These include documents such as brochures, letters and invoices.

Templates are stored as a template file which you load up when you are ready to create a document in the appropriate form. They usually contain logos, page layout and heading information.

Some will even prompt you for information such as name and address. Templates can even present a custom interface with different menu items, icons and commands. You can use this facility to produce a word processing interface with fewer icons, or customised for a particular use in a hospital.

Styles in word processing

Most word processors will allow you to set up multiple styles. They enable the user to match a document to the house style easily. Styles can be used for heading sizes, indenting text, listings, tables and page formats.

Getting data into the system

The biggest problem with any system is **capturing**, or inputting, the data into the system. Time spent typing in data is time not spent dealing directly with patients. There are a variety of ICT options available other than typing data using a keyboard.

Microphones and speech recognition software

A microphone is used as the input device for a speech recognition system. Sound is detected by the microphone and a varying electrical signal is transmitted to the computer. Specialised hardware is used to convert this **analogue** data into **digital** data that can be stored. (For further information on analogue/digital data, see page 115.) Speech recognition software will then convert the words into text in a word processing program.

The main difficulty in a hospital or GP's surgery is that the user must set up the software to recognise his or her voice and speech pattern, but until the software becomes more sophisticated, some words, such as complex medical terms which the software does not recognise, will appear incorrectly on screen.

Speech recognition software works best with a special microphone positioned just centimetres below the mouth, as this avoids picking up surrounding noise or breathing sounds.

Users of speech recognition software may also have to be trained to speak in an appropriate way. Many people find it difficult to speak in a 'writing' style.

Speech recognition software has, however, improved considerably since its developers started to produce software that would listen to whole sentences and phrases rather than individual words. It is now possible to talk directly into a word processor.

Hand-held devices are already being used by doctors working on hospital wards to record voice notes. These could be transferred easily to patients' notes.

A doctor uses a hand-held speech recognition device

A microphone may also be used as an input device to a **voicemail** system. Voicemail uses the Internet to send, store and receive voice messages. These are already available on some mobile phones.

The Internet service provider (ISP – the company providing connection to the Internet) or mobile phone service provider stores the voice message on its server and when the user logs on, the system informs them that they have a voicemail message. The user can then play back the message using a loudspeaker as an output device.

Barcodes and readers

Barcodes are attached to many products, including some medicines, to identify them. Products that are all the same but come in different sizes, for example packets of cereal, have different barcodes.

Barcodes are made up of black lines and white spaces. The barcode shown below is split into two halves, and each half is contained within two thin black stripes which are slightly longer than the rest.

ISBN 0-602-29861-X

9 780602 298616

A barcode

A barcode contains four main pieces of information:

- The country that produced the product (the code for the UK is 50).

- The company that produced the product.

- A code for the product itself, for stock control and pricing.

- A check digit to make sure that the barcode has been read correctly. This is often used to send a beep noise to the till.

Scanners

Barcodes are read by scanners. A scanner is a device used to examine methodically, or scan, a picture, text or other information and send it to the computer as accessible data. The data can then be manipulated in some way before being printed.

Scanners can be classified into two main groups:

- **Hand-held scanners**, such as a gun or a wand – these are moved across the source material being scanned.

- **Flat-bed scanners** – these are more expensive than hand-held scanners. As well as being used at supermarket checkouts to scan in the barcodes of goods sold, flat-bed scanners are used extensively in all contexts where printed data needs to be captured. The source material, a picture for example, is laid on the scanner bed and the device remains stationary while the picture is scanned.

A nurse using a hand-held scanner in a hospital and a flat-bed scanner being used in a supermarket

This type of scanning is very accurate, giving a high range of **resolution** as every dot of a picture is stored. As with video images, however, scanned images take up a lot of disk space.

Scanners work by sending out infra-red laser beams via a set of mirrors, enabling the barcode to be read at lots of different angles. Flat-bed and **horizontal** scanners are the quickest. When an item passes over or under the scanner, the black and white parts are detected by the laser. The black stripes reflect very little light but the white parts reflect the most. This is converted into electrical pulses that are sent along cables to the computer.

Optical mark readers and optical mark recognition (OMR)

Alongside barcodes, other options a designer of a medical ICT system might consider are optical mark recognition (OMR) and optical character recognition (OCR) (see page 21).

Optical mark readers are able to sense marks made in certain places on pre-printed forms. An answer form for a multiple-choice examination provides a good example of an **OMR** form.

The person taking the examination makes a dark pencil mark in the space provided for the answer he or she thinks is right. The printing already on the form is in very pale ink called **fade-out** ink. This is not detected by the mark reader, which will pick up only the dark pencil marks. It does this by detecting the amount of light reflected from different parts of the form.

The dark marks reflect less light. The mark reader transmits data about each space to the computer, and the software works out whether answers are right or wrong, and adds up the total mark.

Mark	A/M	Mark Grid
92	A / M	100 200 00 10 20 30 40 50 60 70 80 90 0 1 2 3 4 5 6 7 8 9
105	A / M	100 200 00 10 20 30 40 50 60 70 80 90 0 1 2 3 4 5 6 7 8 9
90	A / M	100 200 00 10 20 30 40 50 60 70 80 90 0 1 2 3 4 5 6 7 8 9
4	A / M	100 200 00 10 20 30 40 50 60 70 80 90 0 1 2 3 4 5 6 7 8 9
0	A / M	100 200 00 10 20 30 40 50 60 70 80 90 0 1 2 3 4 5 6 7 8 9

A	A / M	100 200 00 10 20 30 40 50 60 70 80 90 0 1 2 3 4 5 6 7 8 9
M	A / M	100 200 00 10 20 30 40 50 60 70 80 90 0 1 2 3 4 5 6 7 8 9

Optical mark recognition data capture form

Other uses of OMR include capturing data from questionnaires, enrolment forms and lottery tickets, and the checking of football pools coupons.

In a health care setting, data capture via OMR forms could form an important part of an ICT system. A large amount of the data required by the system could easily be captured in this way. The advantage of this would be considerable cost savings as all health care staff would not need full access to a computer terminal and could mark an OMR form for later processing.

Activity:

Design a system of patient records that utilises an OMR to capture data.

Optical character readers and optical character recognition (OCR)

An optical character reader also works by detecting the amount of light reflected from a sheet of paper.

A scanner is used with specialised software that transmits data about the pattern of light and dark areas on the paper to the computer, converting the scanned image into standard **ASCII code**. The pattern of data is compared with stored patterns for different characters. The best match is selected and the code representing the character is stored. As each individual letter has been recognised on its own, it can be edited later using word processing software.

OCR software can be used to scan financial documents such as company accounts direct into spreadsheets, as well as to scan text direct into word processors.

OCR technology could be used to capture medical information from traditional paper-based records, but, unfortunately, optical character readers do not work well with handwritten text, as they have to be able to recognise the difference between, for example, an S and a 5, or a B and an 8. It is best if the text is typed, and in a standard font, as different fonts, font sizes and upper and lower case letters may all pose problems. In a health care setting lots of people will have made notes on the patients' record cards. Setting up the system to recognise everyone's handwriting could take longer than typing it all in using a keyboard.

Moving from paper-based systems to ICT systems

ICT has completely changed many traditional working practices in the health service. The unwieldy, often slow, paper-based system has been replaced by word processors, electronic databases, and so on. Some GPs are now linked direct to hospitals and can make bookings and appointments while the patient is in front of them. Electronic records permit instant access to patient information. This is vital in cases where a patient in one part of the country is waiting for a donor organ. As soon as a suitable organ becomes available, the patient must be made ready, and the organ delivered as rapidly as possible for surgery to be effective. Databases of requirements have made this sort of surgery possible.

Activity:

Design a donor organ tracking system based upon a database.

Each organ will have to have an exact match to a specific recipient. Most organs used in transplants are of use for only a very short period of time. Matching the organ to a patient who could be located anywhere in the country is difficult in itself. By adding the dimension of time, any data processing needs to be carried out as rapidly as possible, or the organ will be of no use. As each hospital will have its own records, ensuring that data can be linked to an organ donor database is vitally important.

Activity:

Design a donor card for a young person.

Storing data

A medical ICT system is likely to have a very large amount of data to store. Choosing the correct storage facility, or medium, is an important part of system design.

The commonest types of storage media are **hard disks**, **floppy disks** and **CD-ROMs**. Floppy disks and CD-ROMs are known as backing stores. Backing stores hold data outside the computer's **central processing unit** in some kind of storage medium. When the user wishes to have access to the data, the storage medium must be inserted into a drive in the processing unit, where **read/write** heads transfer the data to main store **RAM**.

Access to backing stores is slightly slower than to main store, but the data held is **non-volatile**. This means it is stored until it is deleted and will not be destroyed if the computer suddenly loses power or develops a fault.

Hard disks

Hard disks and floppy disks are **magnetic storage** media. Data is held as magnetised spots on the disk surface. Magnets need to be kept away from the surface or they can damage the data stored.

A hard disk is made of metal coated with a magnetisable material. It can hold a large amount of data (more than floppy disks) and is usually fixed inside the hard disk drive of the central processing unit (CPU).

The CPU will usually hold several disks on a single spindle. As each disk surface is able to store data, each surface can have its own read/write head. These can operate simultaneously, which means that data can be transferred and utilised more quickly than by using a single larger disk. This access time is very important because modern software often needs to move data to and from a hard disk. It does not hold everything in memory all the time. Therefore, even if the computer has a fast processor, if access time to the hard disks is slow, the software will not run properly.

The read/write heads move across the disk extremely close to the surface. A speck of dust can easily cause damage and for this reason it is normal to seal a hard disk inside the disk drive. This also protects the disk's surface from moisture.

Any loss of data could prove critical in a medical system. Most of the patients' data will be stored on a hard disk. It is also important to back up the data in case anything goes wrong with the system. Hospitals and GPs will also want to transfer data from one system to another. For this, they will need to use a removable medium.

Activity:

Design a back-up system for a hospital computer system or data file.

Floppy disks

Floppy disks used to be the most commonly used removable medium, but they are now being replaced by other removable media.

A computer containing a hard disk drive inside the central processing unit

Hard disks are used to:

- store the **operating system**, **applications software** and user's files for a personal computer

- store the operating system, software and files for a **local area network (LAN)**

- store work awaiting printing.

Inserting a floppy disk into a computer system

Floppy disks are made of plastic coated with a magnetisable material. They are sealed into a protective case with openings to allow data to be written and read. The case can be made of card, but the most commonly used disks have rigid plastic cases. Floppy disks can vary in size, but the commonest is 3.5 inches, which fits into the floppy disk drive of most computers. They hold much less data than hard disks and access is also slower.

Before a floppy disk can be used to store patient data, it must be **formatted**. This creates a magnetic map of the disk surface so that data can be read from the disk or written on to it quickly.

Floppy disks are sometimes used to supply software applications packages to users, but because their capacity is relatively small, each package normally takes up several disks.

It is rare for programs to be run from floppy disks. They are normally installed on to the hard drive first. This makes access much simpler and faster.

Floppy disks are useful for holding patient data files, as long as the files are not too big, and they are used to hold back-up copies of the data and programs on the hard disks. All floppy disks are light and portable, easy to exchange and transport.

A hospital or GP's surgery would normally have lots of patients and therefore a large amount of data to store. For this reason, floppy disks would not be practical to use because lots of disks would be needed. A new generation of floppy disks, sometimes called **super disks**, can hold a larger amount of data. The most common super disks hold 120 megabytes of data.

These could be used in some circumstances.

Zip drives

Special high capacity floppy disks can be used in special drives called Zip drives. These are sometimes also used to back up hard drives or data from databases or other applications. These floppies are slightly larger and twice as thick as normal floppies. They are also used to transfer large files between machines.

A Zip disk and drive

CD-ROMs

CD-ROMs – also known as **optical disks** – work in the same way as compact disks used to store and play music. Data is stored digitally, by changing the way the surface reflects a low energy laser beam. The light is reflected differently according to whether the bit stored is a 1 or a 0. A low intensity beam is used to read the data but a higher intensity beam is needed to write the data on to the disk.

CD-ROM drive

Optical disks have a huge capacity because data can be packed very closely. They are ideal for holding graphics that require large amounts of storage space, such as Clip Art that can be inserted into documents. They can also hold entire encyclopaedias, photographs and all sorts of reference material.

Optical disks are read in the CD drive that forms a standard part of most computer systems. They are more reliable than floppy disks and, because of their great capacity and ease of access, software can be run direct from them without the need to transfer it to the hard drive of a processing unit. If software is held on an optical disk, it does not need to be copied on to another storage medium for back-up purposes.

The main difficulty for a hospital or GP's surgery is that once the surface of a basic optical disk has been altered to store data, it cannot be changed. This means that although these disks can be read many times, they can be written only once. This makes them ideal for storing information on how to treat a medical condition and to store old records, but useless for current patient records that need to be constantly updated.

However, disks that can be written by the user (CD-R), and disks that can be written and read many times over (CD-RW) are also available.

Activity:

Design a CD-ROM to inform patients about a single medical condition.

CD-R

CD-R disks are recordable optical disks. A user can put a blank disk into the CD-R drive and use it to save data or programs. The disk has the same high capacity as a CD-ROM. Write access is not as fast as to a hard disk, but for many uses, this is not important.

The basic CD-R disk can be written only once. It contains a layer of special dye covered by a very thin layer of gold. This, in turn, is covered in a protective plastic coating. When the data is written to the disk, a laser beam is directed on to the dye. The dye absorbs the light and its structure is changed. As a result, the shape of the gold layer changes so that it no longer reflects light when the disk is read. The new shape cannot be altered again. A laser beam is used to read the disk but because it is less powerful than the one required to write the disk, it does not affect the dye and gold, so the disk can be read many times.

CD-R disks are useful for making back-up copies of data files for archiving – that is, files that no longer need to be amended, just stored. They cannot be used to back up data that changes day by day, as in a health care setting. For this, a CD-RW would be more suitable.

CD-RW

CD-RW disks can be written, erased and rewritten many times. They contain a chemical that changes between reflective and non-reflective forms when heated by a high energy laser beam. They are more expensive than CD-R disks and can be used only in a suitable drive.

Unfortunately, CD-R disks cannot be read in a normal CD-ROM drive. This restricts their use to computers with a read-write driver.

Magnetic tape

Magnetic tape used to be a popular medium for backing storage, but is becoming less popular as disks and CDs are developed further. This is largely because of the type of access to data that the different storage media offer. Disks and CDs provide direct access storage. This means any data item on them can be accessed direct without the need to read other data first. Magnetic tape provides **serial access**. All the data before the required item must be read before the required item can be accessed.

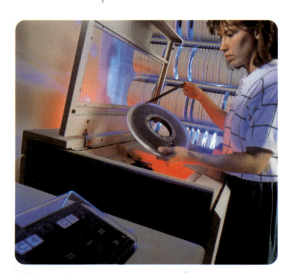

Magnetic tape

Some large computer systems and hospital systems still use large spools of reel-to-reel tape to hold lots of data in storage. The reels fit into large tape drives. An example of magnetic tape still being used is in processing payments of a large hospital. Everyone working for the hospital will have to be paid, so all records will need to be processed. The serial access aspect of magnetic tape will therefore not be a limitation and it will be convenient for the hospital to carry out all wages processing in one huge batch.

In some health care settings, magnetic tape on large spools has been replaced by tape in cartridges that look like audio cassettes, only larger. On all magnetic tape, data is organised into blocks, with interblock gaps between them. A block can often hold several records and there will be end-of-record markers between the records. A block is the amount of data that can be read or written at one time. The interblock gaps allow for starting and stopping the tape in the drive.

Magnetic tape remains useful for keeping back-up copies of data.

Tape streamers are devices that hold a tape cartridge which can be used to back up all the data held on a hard disk. Standard floppy disks would not be suitable for this purpose because their capacity is not great enough.

DVD

Digital versatile disks (DVDs) look like CD-ROMs and can be used to store quantities of data in the same way.

Their capacity is considerably greater than CD-ROMs. For example, a package of applications software stored on six or seven CD-ROMs could be stored on a single DVD.

Some DVDs can store the equivalent of 26 CD-ROMs. DVDs can be used to store applications software, multimedia programs and full-length films. DVDs used to store films produce much better quality pictures and sound than standard video tape. A film stored on DVD can even offer the viewer a choice of language in which the film can be played back.

DVD is being used by the health care profession to record operations. Film can be added to the disk, with notes and annotation. It is even possible to use these disks as a training medium. Trainee doctors can choose from a range of options and simulate the effects on the patient of different key decisions.

DVDs are read in DVD drives, and the most recent generation of DVDs can also be written by the user so that they can be used in much the same way as a hard disk.

● Transferring data

For the health service, one of the main problems with all of the systems described above is that medical records are still available only in one place. Although a patient may be willing to carry a CD-RW containing his or her medical records, a CD is larger than an average pocket.

SMART cards

One answer to the patient record problem, which has already been piloted in a number of countries, is a **SMART card** that will be kept by the patient.

The card will hold all of the patient's medical details and history in a **database** file held on the SMART card. The records are then available to any health care professional treating the patient, even if the patient is away from home. (For more on SMART cards, see pages 93–5.)

Networks

Within a hospital, the transfer of data can take place through a network.

If you use a computer on its own, it is known as a **stand-alone computer**. All communications take place within the machine, or between the various peripheral devices such as monitor, keyboard, printer. The speed of the machine will depend upon the processor speed, location and quality of the components, or parts, used to build the computer.

A stand-alone computer may be ideal for a single dentist or doctor working on his or her own, but transferring files between doctors, nurses and medical centres is difficult.

A stand-alone computer

Two or more computers linked together in the same building, with the aim of sharing data, is called a **local area network (LAN)**.

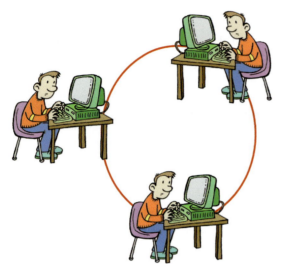

A local area network

Why connect computers together?

The advantages to any organisation of connecting computers together in a LAN are as follows:

- Costly resources such as printers can be shared by all of the computers. This means that better quality printing is available to everyone because one or two expensive, high specification printers can be bought instead of several cheaper, lower specification models.

- A central backing store can be provided in one place – the dedicated **file server** – so all work is saved together. (The file server is normally one computer in the network that has a much higher specification than the others, with a very large hard disk drive. All data

common to the network will be held on the dedicated server. It will also monitor and control the network.) An individual user can load his or her work on any computer on the network.

- Software can be shared, and upgrading is easier too. This gives continuity in the workplace. However, sharing software is often not much cheaper than providing a copy for each machine because a licence has to be bought for each copy of the software needed.

- Data can be shared across the network. For example, this would allow several people to work on the same medical records.

- If the data being shared is in a database, several people will be able to use the database at the same time, but they will not be able to edit the same record at the same time. When a record is opened by one user, it is locked so that other people cannot try to edit it at the same time. This avoids the confusion that would result if several people were trying to edit data at the same time. Once the first user has completed and saved the operation, the record is unlocked again.

- Local e-mail messages can be sent to people working at other terminals on the network. This can save time and ensures that messages get to the right place.

- There may be a local **intranet**. This works like the **world wide web**, with pages of information. The difference is that the pages can be accessed only over the LAN. As it does not involve phone links, an intranet is free.

But there are disadvantages too:

- Where several terminals are served by only one or two printers, long print queues may form, causing people to have to wait for printed output. In a large hospital the printer could be a long way from the terminal or even on a different floor.

- Network security can be a problem, for example medical records are confidential.

- If a **virus** gets into one computer, it is likely to spread quickly across the network because it will get into the central backing store.

- Users of the network must have **user names** and **passwords**. Some users are not very good at keeping passwords secret, or they may use passwords that are easy to guess. Other unauthorised people can then log on to the network.

- If the dedicated file server fails, work stored on shared hard disk drives will not be accessible and it will not be possible to use network printers either.

- Cabling can be expensive to buy and to install. In a busy hospital, cabling must often be placed under the floor or in the ceiling so that people will not trip over it. If connecting cables are damaged, some sections of the network can become isolated. They will not be able to communicate with the rest of the network.

- While the dedicated file server is monitoring and controlling the network, it will not be available for use as an interactive work station.

A network is not simply several computers connected by cables. To connect computers together, a number of hardware and software components, or parts, are needed.

Computer parts found in a typical network

- Network software – this may be part of the operating system, or it can be software designed specifically to manage a network.

- Cables – connecting cables are usually used to connect devices on a network, although some networks make use of radio or microwaves to provide the link. Cables vary in both performance and cost.

- Connectors – these are used to connect network cables to terminals or other devices.

- Network cards – if a personal computer is to be used as a terminal in a network, a device called a network card must be built into it. The network card looks like a small circuit board and slots into one of the connectors on the main circuit board (called the mother board) inside the computer. Network cards have connectors on them for network cables.

Typical hardware devices that may form part of a network are:

- personal computers used as terminals

- one or more central processing units acting as dedicated file servers or print servers

- disk drives
- scanners
- printers
- point-of-sale terminals (in a retail setting).

The planning of the communication links between each of these devices (called **nodes**) must be carried out carefully. There are a number of different ways in which nodes are commonly linked, known as **topologies**. There are four common network topologies:

- **ring**
- **line (bus)**
- **star**
- **hierarchical**.

Ring topology

In a ring topology, all of the terminals or other nodes in the network are connected together in a circle, with no device having any more importance than any other. A disadvantage is that if there is a fault in any part of the circle, all of the nodes will be affected.

A ring topology network

Activity:

Design a network system for use in a hospital.

Line (bus) topology

In this system, data is sent to all nodes on the network at the same time. Devices are positioned along a line, rather like bus stops. As in a ring topology, each device has equal status, but the advantage here is that, if one terminal is not working correctly, the others are not affected. This type of network is cheap and reliable.

Server

A line (bus) topology network

Star topology

In this type of network, a central controller forms the **principal** node, while the **subsidiary** nodes form the points of the star. As the central machine controls the whole system, the whole system will be affected if it breaks down. Star topologies use more cabling than other topologies, and this makes them more expensive. However, communication is fast because there is a direct path from the central controller to each terminal.

Server

A star topology network

Hierarchical network

In a hierarchical network, one or more computers is more powerful than the rest. The relationship between the nodes is called a **client-server** relationship. The more powerful server (or servers) looks after printing, file maintenance and other peripherals. Less powerful computers called clients (or client terminals) are connected to the network. The clients may have no disk drives or processing power of their own. They make use of the functions provided by the server.

There are two types of server in a hierarchical network:

- The file server is used to store both programs and data. It acts as a massive hard drive on behalf of all the client terminals. Where a file server is a dedicated file server, it cannot be used as a terminal and will be occupied all the time in managing the network.

- The print server is a computer in the network that has a printer attached. It manages all print requests from client terminals. The advantage is that the client terminals are not tied up

managing their own printers, but, as mentioned in network disadvantages above, long print queues can sometimes build up.

Transferring files

You could visualise a network as a number of important buildings connected by a road network. The more traffic that uses the roads and the larger the traffic, the slower the system will be.

Of course, it is possible to make the roads wider, or to restrict certain types of traffic at busy times. In computer networks, certain types of cable, particularly cables that incorporate fibre optics, will carry much more traffic than other cables. The term given to how fast the connection will be is bandwidth. A smaller **bandwidth** means the data will flow more slowly than a wider bandwidth.

Hand-held terminals

Within a hospital, **wireless networks** are being used to link **hand-held terminals** direct to patient records. This enables nurses to check drug quantities and treatments accurately as they move around a busy ward.

Paying for the service received

A complication for the health service comes from the way doctors are paid. Payments usually take two forms.

A general payment forms part of any medical funding, but this is usually topped up by what are called 'item of service' payments.

Item of service payments pay for the particular things that doctors do. It is therefore vital for doctors to keep accurate records of whom they see and what they do.

Activity:

Design a spreadsheet that can be used in a doctor's surgery to calculate costs.

Spreadsheets

In an ICT-based environment, payment systems are based upon spreadsheet software. Health care professionals use spreadsheets whenever they are working with numbers, forecasting, or producing accounts, calculations or mathematical models.

All medical treatment has to be fully costed. For private patients, invoices have to be calculated and sent out to the patients, or their insurance companies. For both private and National Health Service patients, accurate records must be kept of drugs, bandages and any other medical items that are used during treatment.

Activity:

Design an invoice system for private patients.

Spreadsheets are sometimes linked to other packages such as databases to keep track of medical resources. Sometimes,

the system is set up to order replacements automatically when stocks get low, or medicines become out of date.

Activity:

Design a system to monitor a range of medical items in terms of use and use-by dates. Your system should include an automatic ordering system when stocks become low.

Before the introduction of ICT and spreadsheets, health care staff, book-keepers, record keepers and accountants used the paper and pencil method along with a ledger or record book containing worksheets. Information and records were stored by hand and financial records were calculated manually and entered into the worksheets. Ledgers were printed with rows and columns that could be used not only for financial records, but also for things like scheduling, employee information, inventory tracking and patient monitoring.

The introduction of ICT has led to the development of software that can store information, perform complex calculations and provide a printed output. This has virtually revolutionised the tasks that can be carried out. The advantages of using a spreadsheet application rather than paper and pencil are numerous – not least of which is that when data is changed, totals and other formulae are automatically recalculated, saving both time and hard work.

Typical medical applications of spreadsheets include:

- displaying, calculating and managing accounts and other financial information

- performing calculations on data collected in experiments and surveys

- producing data from which graphs can be drawn, for example to calculate average temperature for a patient, or to solve a mathematical equation

- costing of treatments.

The software you might use includes: Microsoft Excel, Lotus 123.

Spreadsheet modelling

In a hospital, spreadsheets are used to carry out complex calculations, but they are useful for many other functions. They can be used for **modelling**, allowing the user to ask 'What if?' questions. They can be used in a health care setting to monitor patient progress.

What's in a spreadsheet?

Spreadsheets consist of **rows**, **columns** and **cells**. They are constructed with horizontal rows and vertical columns forming a grid pattern on the screen. The columns are referenced with letters and the rows with numbers. The spaces, or boxes, created by the intersection and spacing of the rows and columns are called cells. Each cell has a unique address called a cell address which refers to the column letter and row number. In the example shown, the framed cell has an address C4.

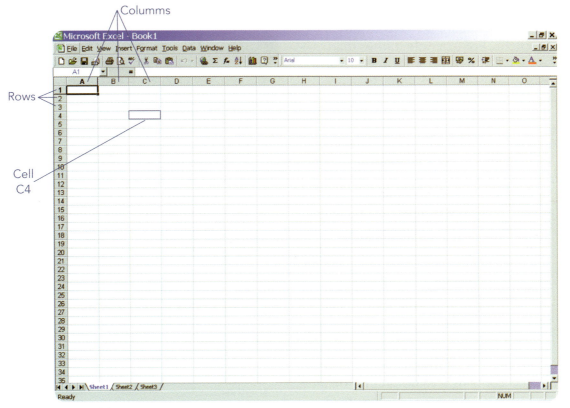

A spreadsheet

Formulae

Words, numbers and formulae can be entered into the cells. A formula can include:

+ for addition

– for subtraction

* for multiplication

/ for division and

^ for exponentiation (powers, for example 4^5 means 4^5).

You can also change the width of columns, duplicate a formula and add borders, headings and colours.

Functions

Most spreadsheets also have a number of functions. For example, rather than listing = B5 + B6 + B7 + B8 + B9 to add up the contents of cells B5 to B9, you can write =SUM(B5:B9).

Other functions include the following:

- AVERAGE – this gives the average of values contained in a range of cells. For example, =AVERAGE(B5:B9) would give the average of the contents of the five cells B5 to B9.

- COUNT – this counts how many cells in a range have data in them.

- IF – this allows for different answers depending on the value in a particular cell. For example, =IF(B5 > =70,"yes","no") would check to see if cell B5 contains a value greater or equal to 70. If it does, it will put 'yes' in the cell, otherwise it will put 'no' in the cell.

Formatting

Data and text can be formatted as in a word processor. You can also use spell checkers, import data from other packages, use macros (see page 18) and **auto-fill functions**, where the spreadsheet will automatically put in items such as dates. This is a useful tool in a health care setting.

Care should be taken to ensure that number cells contain only numeric data if they are to be calculated using formulae.

Cells can also be instructed to operate in a particular mode, for example in sterling (£), or US dollars ($), or to specified numbers of decimal places. A menu provides all the mode options.

Cell referencing

There are two ways of referencing one cell to another in a spreadsheet:

- An **absolute** reference always refers to the same cell on the spreadsheet.

- A **relative** reference refers to a cell that is a certain number of rows and columns away from the current cell. This is important in spreadsheet construction as it means that you can move or copy a cell to a new position and take all of the reference cells with it.

By default, spreadsheet packages use relative cell references. This enables you to copy formulae from one cell to another.

Charts and diagrams

Spreadsheets can automatically generate a range of charts and diagrams. Data from one spreadsheet can also be linked to other spreadsheets, databases, presentation packages and word processing packages.

Lookup tables

You can create lookup tables in spreadsheets. These are often used as validation checks. You type in a unique number such as a patient reference number and, providing that number is one that is stored, the details are automatically displayed. The function for lookup tables in an EXCEL spreadsheet is: = VLOOKUP( ).

Printing spreadsheets

Although spreadsheets have a print option, printing from a spreadsheet application is more complicated than from a word processor. You usually have to define the print range, setting where you want page breaks, which may mean that you have to reduce type size. You may also have to change the paper setting to **landscape** if the **portrait** setting is not wide enough for the spreadsheet.

Presenting the data in a spreadsheet

While formatting the data in a spreadsheet improves its appearance, you will need to consider carefully the use to which your spreadsheet is to be put. If you are the only person going to use it, you probably do not need to spend too much time on its presentation. If it is to be used in a hospital, you will need to consider carefully the clearest and simplest means of presentation to suit the end users. They will not want to be confused or delayed by unnecessary information.

Business graphics programs

Business graphics programs can be used to import sets of data from a database or spreadsheet. Sometimes database and spreadsheet programs have business graphics programs built into them. They offer a choice of graphs including pie charts, bar charts of all kinds, line graphs and x-y or scatter graphs. You can label the graph, the axes and the data, as appropriate. You can also choose from a range of colours and formats to enhance the presentation of graphs and charts. Business graphics software is used to present statistics in a form that can be easily understood, for example, using a pie chart to show the different age groups of population in a town, or using a line graph to show how the price of petrol has increased over a number of years and to sketch mathematical functions.

Help sheet 2: spreadsheets

The content (1) and structure (2) phase are where the scope of the project is decided and plans are made accordingly.

1 Decide on content (what needs to be stored)

- What is the function and purpose of the spreadsheet?
- What does the spreadsheet replace?
- What data do you want to store?
- Type and range of mathematical calculations needed.
- Types of output needed.
- Identify audience – who will use your system?
- Identify context – where and how will your system be used?
- List key points.

2 Structure of spreadsheet

- Look at other examples.
- Identify the *scope* of the project.
- Size, type and range of cells needed.
- Charting and data format requirements.
- Decide upon use of formulae and links.
- Verification and validation checking.
- User interface and screen layout – flowchart possible sequences.
- Navigation interface – buttons, options and icons.
- Who needs to access the data? Access and passwords.
- Backing up the data.

3 Choose hardware and software

Only prototypes of the product are produced in this phase. Once you create anything that will be used in the final product, you have moved into the production phase.

- Select possible hardware platform/software packages for delivery.
- Define user environment/hardware limitations.
- Identify output requirements (screen, web, monitor).

4 Production

You should start to make your system only once you have decided the exact content and goals of the project.

- Create layout and cell size, headings, etc.
- Develop formulae.
- Develop input and output systems.
- Assemble all elements into spreadsheet structure.
- Create/import data:
  - validate and verify.
- Usability test (your response).

5 Evaluation (Does it work?)

- Usability test (user response):
  - calculations, input and output
  - hyperlinks and paste links.
- 'Debug' session.
- Evaluate content or structure that requires modification.
- Revise (at whatever level necessary).
- Produce user documentation.

Databases versus spreadsheets

Deciding when to use a database and when to use a spreadsheet can be difficult. So what is the difference and when would health care professionals choose to use them?

A database organises information on a particular subject for retrieval. Databases consist of one or more tables of information entered by the user to retrieve data for a variety of health care purposes. Data can be retrieved through methods such as asking questions of the data (querying), sorting or filtering, and pulling information into a formatted report, like an invoice, that can be printed. All this makes databases ideal for medical records.

Although the tables in databases look similar to spreadsheets, the tables are used to store raw data. Information in a database is not formatted in the table so there is no need to format the information in the table itself. It is in designing the reports generated from the data in the tables that you need to specify formatting information. This differs from information in a spreadsheet which has to be formatted in the actual spreadsheet.

As discussed earlier, databases use records to structure the tables. A record can contain any number of fields. Reports organise the information in an understandable way and can combine data by performing complex calculations, as with a spreadsheet. Databases can also easily manage a large amount of information and maintain data integrity. For these reasons, databases are much more powerful and manageable, when handling a large amount of information related to a particular topic.

However, most database programs are not as easy to learn as spreadsheet programs and it is not as easy to make structural changes in a database once queries, forms and reports have been developed. Because of this you need to be careful in designing the best way to structure the data into one or more tables before the tables are used to develop a means of retrieving the information.

The reason for this is that once they are saved, queries, forms and reports are all based on the database's table(s). Any changes in a table's structure (such as deleting/changing field names) can cause errors in all the objects based on the changed table. For this reason, when you develop your database you will need a clear vision of all types of data that would need to be included and how to organise it.

An example

Now that you understand the different purposes of databases and spreadsheets, how do you decide which is best for your data? Most hospitals find that using *both* works best. Take a look at the following example:

Hospital A needs a method of storing private patient data related to hospital treatments. The hospital also needs to print invoices and to be able to track invoices and customer contact information. It also needs to be able to calculate quickly what an increase or decrease in treatment prices and/or sales would do to its overall revenue generation, along with a way to analyse trends.

First, the hospital developed a database to store all of its patient information and medical data. It included the following tables: contact information; treatment; and goods used, such as bandages and medicines.

From this, the hospital used the tables and also created queries of the table data on which to base reports, like invoices. Large amounts of data can be stored on the database.

The hospital also created easy-to-use forms for inputting data and a user friendly input interface for easy navigation. This enabled staff to enter data, store data and generate information for invoices, sales by product, sales by patient, and so on in an efficient way. By using a database package, staff could see all the relevant data on one screen, without having to keep scrolling to find information. Several staff can access the data at the same time. There is no difficulty viewing specific patient data sets that they want.

Secondly, the hospital used spreadsheets to calculate quickly by creating various 'What if?' scenarios. These included calculating how changes in price and patient numbers would affect hospital revenue. Staff also used the spreadsheets to generate charts and graphs, allowing them to analyse data in a visual format. Medical data could also be displayed using this facility.

So, using a combination of a database to store its patient records and a spreadsheet to analyse selected information, the hospital achieves the best outcome.

● Extending the network – online systems

Wide area networks

While local area networks are useful within hospitals or GPs' surgeries, the real strength of ICT is the ability to transfer data between locations, indeed across the world. (Where computers are linked over a distance of less than one kilometre, the term used is LAN.) Online systems extend the network still further. The term used for a computer system where the computers are linked across distant locations is a **wide area network (WAN)**. The problems of transferring data now become more complex.

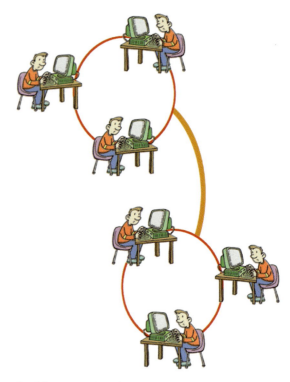

A wide area network

Private networks and virtual private networks

The most expensive, but most secure, online system is to connect different sites of an organisation with its own cabling. This, of course, could mean digging up roads and running cables for several hundred miles. There are a number of companies that sell pre-laid cabling to organisations wishing to purchase this type of service.

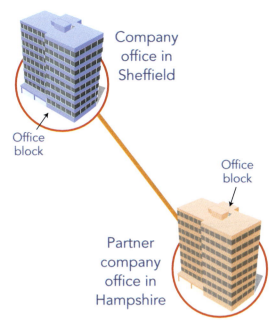

Company office in Sheffield

Office block

Office block

Partner company office in Hampshire

Private circuit connects two sites

Due to the high cost of dedicated lines, most organisations simply rent space on other companies' networks via leased lines, or they use the Internet. This is known as a **virtual private network**. Hospitals often use a virtual private network.

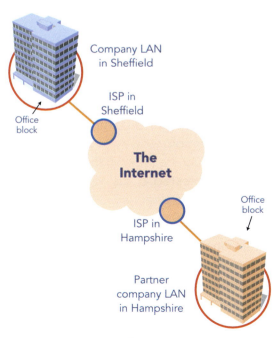

Company LAN in Sheffield

Office block

ISP in Sheffield

The Internet

Office block

ISP in Hampshire

Partner company LAN in Hampshire

A virtual private network

The Internet

Organisations that deal with other companies and people at home use the Internet to obtain a worldwide presence, with each user accessing the network in different ways from **modems** to dedicated lines.

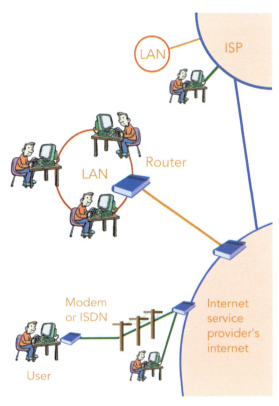

LAN

ISP

Router

LAN

Modem or ISDN

Internet service provider's internet

User

Using the Internet to obtain a worldwide presence

Access speeds will differ according to the bandwidth and type of access the various users of the system have. Sometimes the modem will restrict access; at other times the cause will be the bandwidth. The main difficulty home users have is that Internet service providers will often sell the bandwidth to a large number of end users in the hope that not too many people will connect at the same time.

Use of ICT in the health care services

Online medical support and information

The Internet has opened up a vast source of information, both for health care professionals and patients.

There are sites run by patient groups, specialist units (like the National Institute of Health in the USA) and charitable societies, such as the RNIB, where patients can find out information on a variety of complaints.

Doctors can use the Internet to keep up to date with the latest drugs and treatments, using a web-based drugs dictionary and online medical support. PCS Health Systems has developed an online network of over 54 000 pharmacies and 50 000 doctors in the USA. Whenever a patient needs a prescription or visits a doctor, the system searches its patient records. It checks what prescriptions the patient has had in the past and any allergies recorded by any doctor or pharmacy on the network. If the patient is likely to have an adverse reaction to a drug, the system flags this up. It also states what other drugs the patient is taking and notifies the doctor if there is a likelihood of the combined effect being a problem. Doctors who use the system say that in one year alone the system noticed 45 million possible dangerous interactions of which five million could have killed the patient.

Activity:

Design a medical Internet site to give patients information about a medical condition.

Activity:

Design a printed leaflet to inform patients about a particular medical condition.

Using directories and search engines

Using search engines on the Internet is becoming increasingly important as a means of finding reliable, good quality information. It is not just the medical profession that needs to make use of this technology.

There are hundreds of search engines available but very few people have been trained to use them. Although we often refer to all search devices on the Internet as search engines, there are two types of systems in use:

- directories such as Yahoo
- search engines such as AltaVista and Infoseek.

A directory is a catalogue of sites. Directories are often called subject 'trees' because they start with a few main categories and then branch out into subcategories, topics and subtopics. A directory is a good starting point to find information. However, you may not find what you are looking for if the topic you are interested in has not been included in the directory.

Directories are also useful for finding information on a topic when you don't know exactly what you need. Many large directories include a key-word search option which usually removes the need to work through many levels of topics and subtopics.

Because directories cover only a small fraction of the pages available on the Internet, directories are most effective for finding general information on popular or scholarly subjects. If you are looking for something specific, use a search engine.

Search engines are very different from subject directories. While people organise and catalogue directories, search engines use specialised software to scan the Internet looking for information on Web pages and storing that information in gigantic databases. The software uses bots, spiders and crawlers to log the words on each web page. You should always try more than one search engine as they all contain different sites, and an engine that is up to date one day may be out of date the following week.

With a search engine, key words related to a topic are typed into a search 'box'. The search engine scans its database and returns a file with links to websites containing the word or words specified. Because these databases are very large, search engines often return thousands of results. Without search strategies or techniques, finding what you need can be like finding a needle in a haystack.

To use search engines effectively, you will need to use special techniques to narrow results and push the most relevant pages to the top of the results list. Below are a number of strategies for boosting search engine performance.

Knowing what to ask for

One of the biggest problems that people searching the Internet have is asking for the information they want in the right way.

When we look at a book or other published material, we can scan the pages until we see what we want. Knowing what we want when we see it is easy. On the Internet, we have to put in search words. These words have to be specific.

If the search words are too general, the user may be faced with hundreds of websites which would take time to look through, and much of which might not be relevant. Search engines simply display links to web pages that contain the search words. However intelligent the search engine, it cannot work out what the user really means.

To use search engines effectively, you need to think of search terms or key words. Professional users of the Internet spend time planning ahead. They consider the key words for the information they want to find, often listing these on paper. This enables them to consider synonyms, or words similar in meaning to their key words. This is necessary because a website might use different terms to describe its content than the ones first listed.

Another problem revolves around the international nature of the Internet. We all have subconscious knowledge. Most of you will know the term ICT, but this term is not used by most people outside the UK. Effective searches on the Internet use words and language that are universal.

As well as knowing what you want, you need to think about what you do not want. Some of the better search engines allow you to tell them what you do not want, as well as what you do. This is usually achieved by placing a – (minus) sign in front of the words you do not want.

Common symbols for using search engines

There will usually be a choice of search engines that can be accessed through the search button on the toolbar.

Given the same starting information, each of these may produce different results because they search in different ways. A search engine will normally request key words to describe what a user is looking for and there are several ways of searching:

- If you type in the key words **broken legs**, a search engine will search for all documents that contain **broken** and/or **legs**, giving highest priority to those that contain both words. This could result in a long and confusing list of possible websites.

- If only lower case letters are used, the search will find documents that contain the words regardless of whether they are in lower or upper case. If a mixture of upper and lower case is specified, the search will try to find words that match the words exactly – **Broken Legs**.

- By placing double quotation marks around the phrase, this will make sure that the search engine finds only the documents where the words appear in that order.

Advanced searches

Search criteria are used to reduce the length of the list of websites produced, but it will still often be necessary to use more precise search instructions, that is, carry out an **advanced search**.

Search engines have slightly different requirements for carrying out advanced searches. The general rules are as follows.

+ and –

By placing a + (plus) in front of a word, documents will be found that contain that word. For example:

- +broken+legs will find all documents that contain the word broken and also the word legs

- broken+legs would give a list of documents that contain the word legs but will not necessarily be about being broken.

If you put a – (minus) in front of a word, documents will be found that do not contain that word. For example, +broken–legs would give a list of documents that contain the word broken but miss out those that contain legs.

AND, OR and AND NOT

The word AND can be used to combine key words. All words joined by AND must be contained in the document for it to be listed in the results of a search.

OR can be used to combine key words. At least one of the words joined by OR must be contained in the document for it to be listed in the results of the search. OR is often used to link words that have a similar meaning in a search, for example jam OR marmalade.

AND NOT is also used to combine key words. The search will not include documents containing the word following AND NOT. For example jam AND NOT marmalade would produce documents relating to jam, but none containing the word marmalade.

Brackets

Brackets are used in searches in the same way as they are used in mathematics. They can group words together to make a more complex search possible. For example, horses AND (dogs OR cats) would produce a list of documents containing the word horses and either the word dogs, or cats, or both.

Wild card

The character * (asterisk) is called a wild card and can be used to stand for any character or set of characters. For example, typing auto* would produce a list of documents containing words such as automobile, automatic, autogiro, autopsy and so on.

Titles

Rather than searching whole documents or web sites for key words, a search can be limited to the titles of documents or websites. If the words are important to the document or website, they may well be contained in the title. The search engine is instructed to do this by typing t: before the key word(s). For example, t: "fuel shortage" would search titles containing those words, in that order.

● Use of the Internet by the health services

When considering Internet use by the health services, we need to bear in mind that there are two types of information published on the Internet. The first type relates to information that is suitable for health care professionals. The second type is aimed at patients and the general public.

If you are using a search engine to find information relating to the health services, you will need to be aware of this.

It is already possible to search for references to medical conditions and, as a patient, compare the types of treatment that different doctors have offered. It is even possible to access some of the information sources that doctors themselves have used. Although in the main this is considered to be a good thing, it has a disadvantage. Not all of the information available on the Internet is of a high quality. At worst, patients could be put in danger and doctors could have an increased workload spending time discussing with patients inaccurate information they have found on the Internet.

These are some of the types of information available on the Internet:

- health promotion, including all sorts of sites ranging from how to give up smoking to eating a healthy diet

- data about diseases, including information about Aids, cancers and most common diseases across the world

- treatments and procedures – these sites offer information to both doctors and patients and are often written in non-technical language

- useful documentation – these sites often contain online versions of patient leaflets and handouts

- patient support, including mailing lists, newsgroups and a wide variety of online chat facilities where patients can talk to people with similar complaints

- searchable databases, particularly related to pharmaceuticals.

Searching for information on the health services

The health services have a number of dedicated search engines, including OMNI, Medical Matrix and Health on the Net. There are even virtual hospitals with huge collections of lecture notes, tutorials and other teaching materials. You can also search for pharmaceuticals companies, official health organisations, health associations, regulatory bodies and for clinical trial information.

Using e-mail

E-mail is another important facility offered by the Internet. It is a method of sending messages from one **terminal** to another via a communications link.

As with all other **computer functions**, you need the appropriate software. You also need an **e-mail account**, which is usually supplied by the Internet Service Provider that you use. You have to pick an **e-mail address**, which must be different from anyone else's address. To send a message, you need to know the e-mail address of the person you are sending it to.

The **software** provides the **interface** for writing and addressing the message. It also displays **messages received**, and provides functions such as an **address book** and **diary**. Messages can be written, and any documents **attached** to them, while the computer is **off-line**. This helps to keep costs down. Telephone charges are only incurred while actually sending and receiving messages.

The sent message is placed in a **mail box** on a main computer. As soon as the person to whom you have sent the message **logs on** (**connects** his or her computer system to the Internet), she can access the mail box and, when the incoming message has been transmitted to the **Inbox**, she can read the message.

Control technology

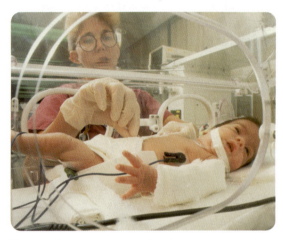

The incubator uses control technology to monitor the baby

A modern hospital uses some of the latest control equipment to monitor a patient's vital signs and to distribute accurate quantities of drugs. There is a large number of opportunities within the health service to use control systems. For example, premature or sick newborn (neonatal) babies can be cared for using the following:

- A skin temperature monitor for a baby in an incubator passes information back to the control unit, which adjusts the air temperature in the incubator according to the needs of the baby.

- A neonatal monitor registers the baby's breathing and heartbeat.

This system can activate an alarm if there is a change in either function. A neonatal ventilator controls oxygen supply to the baby's lungs.

- An electronic infusion device feeds the baby and administers drugs in precisely measured amounts, intravenously.

- An alarm monitors the baby's movement and can warn medical carers if the baby fails to breathe.

There are many other electronic devices in use, including weighing machines and nasal tubes.

Activity:

Design one control system that could be used in a newborn baby unit.

Introducing ICT systems

Issues surrounding the introduction of ICT systems to the health service include:

- the need for training

- a shift in responsibility, for example a receptionist in a hospital takes on the vital responsibility of ensuring that data is accurate

- a need for confidentiality and data security.

A dental surgery

The modern dental surgery contains a wide range of new technology. Alongside electronic dental equipment, patient records have also been computerised. ICT systems help to ensure that each patient is allocated the right amount of time for treatment.

With dental work charged both by the minute and for the resources used, tracking precise times and costs is essential. Added to this, a range of patient options from the National Health Service, insurance-based schemes and private care are available. Each scheme has its own pricing structure.

Activity:

Devise a database booking system for a dentist.

Activity:

Devise a user friendly pricing system for a dental practice.

Ideally, patients should attend for a regular check-up every six months. Most dental practices send out a reminder letter.

Activity:

Design a system to send out a reminder letter to patients.

When carrying out a dental examination, it is important that the dentist has accurate records of previous treatments.

Activity:

Devise a patient database.

Use of ICT in the entertainment industry

Think about the types of entertainment you enjoy, and where they take place. Sporting facilities, leisure centres, nightclubs, restaurants, theatres and the home are just some of the places where you can take part in entertainment.

● Theatres

Theatre set and control desk for a technically challenging theatre production where two adjacent theatres and one group of actors are staging linked plays simultaneously

Before exploring the use of ICT in theatres, let's first define the term theatre. A theatre can be used to describe both a performance, and the building in which the performance takes place. The type of performance can also vary, from cinema,

through modern music and opera, to drama. All utilise ICT to manage data and ensure that information is available in the right place at the right time.

The term theatre may describe:

- ● theatre buildings without theatre companies (actors/actresses, etc.)
- ● theatre buildings with theatre companies
- ● theatre companies without buildings

as well as the performance that takes place.

Although theatres are about live performances on a stage rather than on a **display screen** or **television**, computers are used throughout the theatre.

● From stage to screen

Every desktop computer, most portables, electronic calculators and mobile phones have a display screen of some kind. On a desktop computer, the screen is often known as the monitor, or as a VDU (visual display unit). Screens are available in various sizes. Display screens used in ICT applications are called monitors.

Theatre booking offices use monitors to enable actors and stage staff working behind the scenes to view performances, together with a wide range of other uses such as to display ticket availability.

Standard VDUs on desktop computers work in the same way as the screen on a standard television set, but this technology is too bulky for portables or hand-held devices. These use liquid crystal displays, made from flat plates with liquid between them. Although this system takes up much less space, the disadvantage is that these screens can be viewed only from a limited angle. As the technology improves, flat screen panels are becoming available for desktop computers too.

A screen display is either **monochrome**, or **colour**. Monochrome does not necessarily mean black and white. This may be orange or green text on a black background, the significant difference being that such screen displays do not provide the range of colour of a colour screen.

Monochrome screens are suitable where they are used only to provide text displays. Colour is considered to be more restful to the eye and is necessary to show detail of graphics, or to highlight error messages, menu options, etc. in word processing. However, the use of colour takes up more storage space and requires more processing time.

The **resolution** of a monitor, or screen, is very important. This relates to the clarity of the image on the screen and is defined by the number of separate units of light (known as **pixels**) across and down the screen that can be displayed. A pixel is square in shape and represents the smallest area of the screen which the computer can change. For some applications, such as **computer aided design (CAD)** and **desktop publishing**, a high resolution screen is required, or images will not be sufficiently clear.

The higher the resolution of a display, the more pixels are used. This takes up more storage space in the computer. High resolution images also take longer to process and a fast processor is required to animate a high resolution picture smoothly.

The screens used to monitor a performance will be of high resolution. Screens used to book tickets do not need to have such high resolution.

It is possible to use a method called **interlacing** to produce a screen image that seems to have a higher resolution than the screen can display. However, this results in more screen flicker than a display that has not been interlaced.

Desk space

Desk space is important in a crowded box office, as it is in many other modern office settings. To save space, flat screen monitors are sometimes used. These take up very little desk space and can even be hung on a wall.

The flat screens that are now becoming available offer better quality with less flicker, and they take up less space. They are, however, more expensive.

The main disadvantage of screens as output devices is that they do not provide permanent copy. They are also unsuitable for any users with visual problems. Advantages are that they provide high speed change of display, which can include text, graphics and colours. They make no noise and do not waste paper.

Taking the booking

For most theatre monitoring situations, no hard copy is needed. Ticket booking is of course an exception to this.

Theatre bookings are often taken over the telephone. The booking office needs to check ticket availability first on a VDU or monitor. This is sometimes achieved by selecting from a menu, often using a **touch sensitive** screen.

Taking a theatre booking

Touch sensitive screens

This is a screen through which data can by entered into a computer by touching it with a finger. Items are selected as they would be with a mouse or light pen. Touch sensitive screens usually work by means of criss-crossing beams of infra-red light just in front of the glass. When the user touches the glass two sets of rays are blocked giving an X and Y axis. Most interactive whiteboards work in a similar way to this.

Touch sensitive screens are ideal in theatres, museums, shops and Internet booths. They are easy to use. They are also ideal for information kiosks. The advantage of a touch screen is that no extra **peripherals** (other pieces of kit such as a mouse) are needed, just the monitor, although this has to be adapted to respond to touch. The touch method is very useful in situations where a keyboard or mouse could become dirty or wet, and where users are standing and moving about and where limitations on the number of options available are required.

Forecasting costs

One of the main uses of ICT in a theatre is in administration. It is used to control and forecast (predict) costs and revenue. This activity is known as theatre finance. When considering the finances involved in the running of a theatre, you need to think about earned income and non-earned income. Non-earned income often forms a large part of opera and drama income. It comes in the form of funding from organisations like the Arts Council and National Lottery Fund which provide support for the arts. Without this funding, many live productions would not take place.

A theatre seat, whether for live or filmed performance, is like an aircraft seat. The value of the seat disappears completely when the performance starts. Seats in theatres can be described as the ultimate dated perishable goods. These seats cannot be left in the fridge for sale the following day. One of the main tasks of any theatre management is to try to ensure the sale of as many seats as possible prior to the performance. Theatre seats are sold through what is called a box office. Prices of seats often vary according to where someone sits in the theatre and when and how people buy their tickets. Often the theatre will have special offers to fill as many seats as possible. Many theatre companies reduce the price of any remaining seats just before the performance. Any amount of money received is better than an empty seat.

Activity:

Design a ticket-issuing system for a theatre.

Activity:

Design a database for use in a theatre. Your database must show ticket sales and prices by seat and performance.

Box office income is one of the most variable figures in theatre finance. Predicting potential sales is a major problem for all theatre companies. While seat prices form an essential part of income received, there are a large number of other sources of income. These include sales of programmes, ice creams, drinks, food and, in cinemas, computer games.

Unfortunately, all of these additional sources of income are dependent upon the number of people attending the theatre, that is, upon ticket sales. Low seat sales also have other disastrous effects. The image of the theatre suffers as audiences assume that the theatre, play or film cannot be much good if nobody goes.

Activity:

Design a spreadsheet to show and forecast box office and additional income.

Theatre seat prices rarely relate to actual costs. For some productions, this would make seat prices too high. Seats are sold at the highest price that the market will bear – in other words, at the highest price that people are willing to pay. People attending theatres do not only have to pay for the ticket. They have to pay for their transport, refreshments and any other associated costs. Seat prices need to be flexible from one production to another. Theatres often carry out an analysis of the effectiveness and cost of other similar attractions.

Activity:

Devise a system to evaluate costs and effectiveness of a range of similar theatre productions.

The number of seats sold is called the rate of occupancy. It is usually calculated as a percentage. If a theatre works on the basis of an occupancy rate of 70–75 per cent when calculating income, any occupancy (seats sold) over this percentage will be a bonus. You should note, however, that any party reductions, subscriptions, special offers, etc., must be taken into consideration before income can be calculated. As some theatres charge different prices according to where the seats are, the *type* of seats occupied can make a big difference to income.

Unfortunately, this means tickets need to be printed on an individual basis. Each ticket needs to show the seat number, date and time of the performance and price. If the seat is sold as a special offer to an individual, it could also show the purchaser's name. As each seat is sold, a database needs to keep track of this, so that a seat is not sold more than once.

Once a ticket is booked on the system, a hard copy is needed. This will be sent to the customer making the booking. The hard copy is achieved by outputting the booking to a printer.

Printers

Printers produce output in the form of permanent copy, normally on paper. Many can also print on to acetate sheets that are used on overhead projectors.

There are three main types of printers:

- **impact** (including dot matrix and golf ball)
- **inkjet**
- **laser**.

Although theatres use special ticket printers, many of which use thermal printing methods, most of the printers in a theatre work in a similar way to the printers you will have at school or college.

Impact printers

Dot matrix printers

Dot matrix printers were the first type to be developed for use in computer systems. They are impact printers, producing output by hammering pins or character patterns against a ribbon and the paper. This means that they are able to print multi-part stationery such as invoice sets used by many companies, where a number of copies are required.

Dot matrix printers are noisy and produce a low quality of printout and,

for these reasons, have largely been replaced by either inkjet or laser printers.

Golf ball printers

Golf ball printers use a rotating sphere of letters to produce high quality printout. They are suitable only for printing alphanumeric characters and cannot produce graphics. Their advantages are good quality of output and the ability to print multi-part stationery.

Non-impact printers

Inkjets and lasers are non-impact printers. They are quiet when working and produce high quality output. Both can produce graphics and most types are capable of producing colour.

Inkjet printers

Inkjet printers are often called **bubble-jets** because they produce output by spraying tiny drops of ink on to the paper. The print head of an inkjet printer consists of nozzles through which ink flows and is heated, to form bubbles. Each bubble expands and breaks, releasing a tiny ink droplet. The dots formed are smaller and more numerous (usually between 300 and 800 dots to the inch) than those produced by a dot matrix printer.

Inkjet printers work well on ordinary paper, giving high quality output.

Standard inkjet printers have three-colour **cartridges** – cyan (blue), magenta (red) and yellow – plus a black cartridge. Inkjet printers designed to produce photographic quality output have five-colour cartridges, plus black.

Colour inkjet printers can produce images that are almost as good as photographs if they are printed on high quality paper. The inkjet system does not work well, however, on any paper that is absorbent as the wet ink droplets tend to spread before they can dry.

Inkjets are slower than laser printers but less expensive to buy. Running costs are also usually higher than for lasers as high quality printing paper is costly and ink cartridges, especially colour cartridges, can be expensive and do not last long under certain conditions of use.

Inkjet printers normally take up less space than laser printers and are almost silent in operation.

Laser printers

A laser printer uses a laser beam to build up an electrical image of a page on a light sensitive drum in the same way as a photocopier. The image is built up from dots. Early laser printers used 300 dots to the inch, but the latest printers use at least 600 dots to the inch (2.5 cm) so that the individual dots cannot be seen. Once the image has been formed on the drum, a plastic powder called toner is held against the paper in the same pattern. The paper and toner are heated to fix the powder to the paper.

Colour laser printers use three-colour **toner** cartridges plus a black cartridge.

Laser printers are fast and produce high quality output. They are expensive, however, particularly colour laser printers. Toner cartridges have to be replaced as soon as they run out and may also be expensive. Some suppliers operate schemes for recycling used toner cartridges.

● Secondary sources of income in a theatre

Programmes

The marked-up draft of the first page of a theatre programme and the final version

Souvenir programmes are usually designed using a desktop publishing (DTP) software package. Word processors can also be used to publish documents. They can often be used to carry out most of the DTP functions. Commercially, professional DTP programmes produce higher quality and printer-ready files.

Programmes should be regarded as a service to the audience. They should, therefore, contain information about the performance and its background. Programmes are often bought as a souvenir. A careful balance between images and text is vital. A programme is also a useful place for a theatre to promote forthcoming attractions.

Most souvenir programmes are sold in the UK to make money for a theatre. In the United States, it is common practice to give away programmes free of charge as part of the ticket price. Many of the programmes in the major theatres of Europe are also free as they are paid for by advertising.

Desktop publishing

Desktop publishing can be used to produce high quality pages that combine text and graphics. It allows the user to rearrange parts of a page to achieve the effect that is required.

The theatre company will want to produce an attractive leaflet to encourage people to buy a ticket. The company is likely to include pictures of the stars of forthcoming productions, eye-catching graphics and a brief description of planned shows.

Desktop publishing requires a computer with a high specification. The computer needs a large amount of **RAM (random access memory)** and a fairly large hard disk to store **digital** pictures in high resolution. The computer system will also need a good quality monitor, high quality colour printer and a range of other devices such as scanner and digital camera.

The types of software you might use include: Aldus PageMaker, Front Page, InDesign, Microsoft Publisher.

There are many different types of desktop publishing software available. There will be no single best program. However, specific programs are better suited to certain tasks than to others. Some of these are discussed below.

Page layout software

Single-page layouts or short documents that combine text and graphics require page layout software that provides extensive typographic control and graphics handling capabilities. The theatre would use this type of software for advertisements, flyers, brochures, newsletters, posters and business cards.

Long document composition

Books and large documents such as stage scripts require a program that can handle repeating items such as headers and footers. They also need a program that can produce tables of contents and indexes, insert page numbers and integrate items such as data from spreadsheets or databases. Extensive text handling facilities, such as pagination and the full automation of repetitive tasks, are needed for this type of software.

Database assisted publishing

These software packages are designed to handle the importing and formatting of external data through what are called 'front ends'. They are used mainly for catalogues, price lists and directories.

Corporate publishing

The theatre will produce programmes, marketing and promotional material using corporate publishing packages. These desktop publishing packages are particularly suited to high quality typesetting and document composition.

Home publishing

Desktop publishing packages designed for home use contain a large number of templates, design wizards, font ranges and Clip Art collections. They do not, however, produce the high quality typesetting and printout needed for a professional theatre. They are ideal for producing things like greeting cards, banners, posters and photo albums.

Using a DTP package

DTP packages make full use of **drop down menus**. These are usually controlled by a mouse or pointer such as a **light pen**.

Using a mouse

The theatre will probably use a mouse to select from the options offered in the desktop publishing package.

A mouse is used on the desktop and translates its movements over a flat surface into digital information.

In a traditional mouse, the ball underneath rotates as the mouse is moved, and sensors pick up the movement. More modern types of mouse use a beam of light instead of a ball to monitor movement.

The information gained from the movement is fed to the computer, causing the cursor to move on the screen. Mice usually have one, two or three buttons that are used to make selections on the screen.

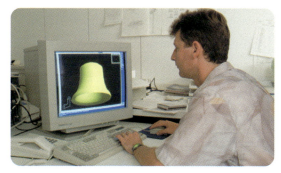

A designer uses a mouse to design a three-dimensional object in a CAM package

A mouse may be used to select options from a menu or from a set of icons, to position the cursor when editing text or using design software, to select an object in a drawing or a block of text to be copied, moved or deleted. It is ideal for use with a desktop computer, typically in an office, but is not practical for use with a portable computer such as a laptop, notebook or palmtop model. In these cases, the cursor is moved by a 'static' mouse encapsulated within the keyboard and operated from it, or by touching the screen with a **light pen**. Special software is required to make light pens work. Point and touch methods are mainly used for design work.

A hand-held personal organiser using a touch screen and pointing device

Tracker ball

A tracker ball is like an upside-down mouse. The user rotates the ball but the 'mouse' part stays still. Both tracker balls and track pads take up less space than a mouse and normally form an integral part of a portable computer.

Joystick

A joystick is similar to a tracker ball but does not form an integral part of the computer. When the lever is moved, the cursor moves in a similar direction on the screen. The lever can be moved in any direction from its zero position. It can also be made to produce faster movements on the screen by pushing it further from the zero position. Like the mouse, a joystick usually has buttons with which actions can be carried out once the cursor is in the right place. Examples of how joysticks are used are with computer games and with ultrasound scanners in hospitals.

Help sheet 3: desktop publishing

1 Message (decide on content)
- What do you want to say?
- Identify audience – who will use your document?
- Identify context – where will your publication be read?
- Choose/compose text.
- Choose/compose graphics.

2 Image (decide on overall look of finished document)
- Look at other examples.
- Number of pages, size of pages.
- Page layout – how many pictures, house style?
- Produce paper and pencil mock-ups.
- How will the paper be folded?
- Identify the range and scope of the project.

3 Choose hardware and software
- Decide on software package to use at this point to ensure compatibility of word processing files and graphics.
- Decide on the hardware you wish to use.
- Determine output requirements (printer, paper, resolution, colour).

4 Production
- Format page, titles, headers, columns, font.
- Enter and format text.
- 'Place' graphics and images.
- Test output and revise.
- Final colour output.

5 Evaluation (does it work?)
- Usability (readability) test.
- Evaluate content or structure to see if it works or requires modification.
- Revise (at whatever level necessary).

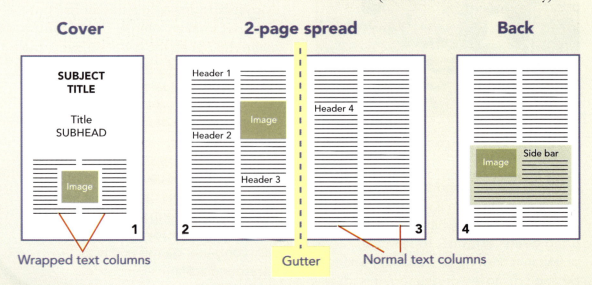

Page layouts

Using design to communicate

Modern software programs allow companies to create attractive page layouts for their documents and websites. From annual reports to packaging design to multimedia presentations, it seems possible to create millions of designs in millions of colours in a wide variety of typefaces, using artwork and unusual graphic elements. If you surf the web, you will find all sorts of text effects such as type that blinks or sparkles, pages that push and pull viewers all over the web, pages that shout at their viewers and are hard on the eye. But there are also a lot of very well designed pages.

Just because it is possible, though, doesn't mean you should do it. In design, there are rules about what's good and what's not good – and the best part is that it is perfectly all right to break them! But to be able to break the rules of good design, a designer should first learn them and get to know them well.

Before the theatre starts to design its printed publications or website, it must think about the documents its customers read and the places on the Internet that they like to visit. Its designers will look at the pages that receive a lot of visitors or attract comment. They will think about the magazines and newspapers their customers buy, and explore standard page layouts. They might find that some of the answers are in the layout of rival theatres. What makes a page stand out in the customer's eye? How easy is it to follow the website links to navigate around a site?

Before communication between theatre and customers can begin, the publication or website must first catch the attention of the reader or viewer. Communication and the impression made by any websites, documents and reports are improved by good design. Good design is based upon an understanding of page layout and the use of type and graphics.

To develop their communication skills, designers look at existing good practice and practise controlling the basic functions of the software to improve the presentation of text and graphics on their pages.

Visually, there is very little new in design. Most designers of web pages and printed materials take their ideas from other documents and rearrange them to suit their own needs. No matter how simple the design may be, there are certain principles or rules that must be followed. **Layout** is the process of arranging the text, pictures and other graphics on the page.

Before designers start to design a document they need to consider the following:

- Objective of the communication. What is the purpose of the finished product? Is it to sell, to inform or for reference?

- Target group. Will the material be for personal use, for a particular group of people such as scientists, for teenagers, etc? The design approach would be different for each. The theatre might want to reach a certain part of its audience, or people who have never visited the theatre before.

- Personality of the communication. Should it be sophisticated, gaudy, dignified, humorous, or have some other quality? The type of paper, typography and illustrations depend on these decisions.

- Style of the finished document, presentation or website. Will it contain photographs? Will it be typographic (text only), or will it contain cartoons, illustrations, or both?

- Layout format. Will the product be a booklet, folder, bulletin, brochure, pamphlet, or an entire book? The theatre's budget is likely to affect decisions of style and layout. Some products will be much more expensive than others.

- Approximate trimmed dimensions. What will be the size of the document? This will affect the size of standard paper that can be used or the screen resolution to be used.

- Approximate number of pages. Will there be one sheet printed on only one side or on both sides? Will the communication be designed for a website or mobile phone? If on paper, will a sheet be printed on both sides and folded? Will there be several pages?

- If printed, approximate number of copies. The number of copies required often determines the printing process used.

- Layout required. Does the customer want to see thumbnail sketches, a rough layout and a comprehensive layout?

The designer will use white space – empty space with nothing printed on it – not cramming everything on to a page with no room to breathe. White space allows different elements on a page to stand out. A page with no white space can be intimidating – the reader doesn't know where to start reading and may not want to read it at all. White space, of course, doesn't have to be white; it can even be black, but its effect may not be so stark if it is actually a pattern or colour. Also, the designer will not want to 'trap' white space on the middle of a page with no outlet, no way to escape to the edge of the page – that acts against the feeling of 'breathing space'.

Balance

At the heart of good design is the arrangement of one or more items of text or graphics so that, visually, they equal each other. Every object in nature has structural balance, from the symmetry of a flower petal to the complexity of a snail's shell. The balance needed every time we perform any form of physical movement is automatically maintained by a built-in equilibrium. It stops us falling over. All made structures, even if not equal on all sides, must maintain a balance.

For graphic design, the visual centre of any typical page is not the actual physical centre but what is called the optical centre. This visual point of balance can be worked out mathematically as being three-eighths from the top of the page (or five-eighths from the bottom).

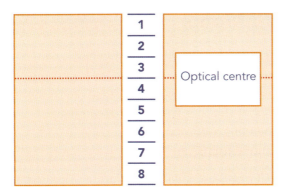

The mathematical balance of a page

Balance is achieved on a page by the margins – the amount of white space surrounding printed or web-based pages. These affect both appearance and the readability of the document. The default settings of most word processors create a margin of one inch at each edge of the page. The designer may try increasing side margins (say, to one-and-a-half inches). This improves the appearance of work on the page. Wide margins indicate luxury or formality; narrow margins indicate business.

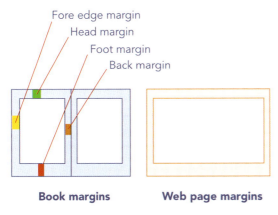

Fore edge margin
Head margin
Foot margin
Back margin

Book margins **Web page margins**

Book and web page margins

The width of the margins used depends upon the document being produced. Two facing pages of a book are seen as a single unit; the inside (back) margins are always smaller than the outside (fore edge) margins.

Books and magazines are designed differently from single-page documents. When a book is opened, any two pages next to each other must appear to belong together.

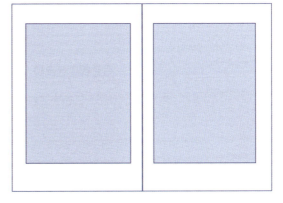

Standard margins

Balance can also be achieved by text justification:

Full justification arranges the text in a straight line on both the left and right-hand margins.

Centre-justified text is ragged on both sides but symmetrical in the centre of the page.

Left-justified text is straight only on the left, leaving the text ragged on the right. This has the advantage of producing more regular word spacing, but full justification often has a better visual effect overall.

Right-justified text is straight only on the right, leaving the text ragged on the left.

Symmetrical balance

Any symmetrical layout is likely to produce a more static, restful design. However, because a centred layout is so static, it is very easy to make it pleasing to look at but rather boring.

Formal (symmetrical) balance is pleasing but boring

One of the major advantages of an asymmetrical (not symmetrical) layout is that it is more lively. If the theatre wants to give the impression that it is innovative and lively, its designers may choose an asymmetrical layout for promotional material.

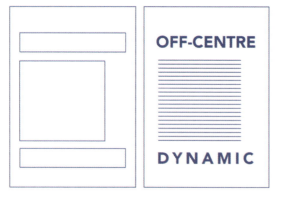

Informal (asymmetrical) balance creates visual interest

Columns

The designer must show how he or she intends to divide the page, or pages, into text and graphics. At this stage decisions about the font types and size of main heading and subheadings, column widths and margins can be made.

All pages are split into columns. The first column is usually for the border and the second column is for the text. Sometimes the text fits into one column like a book. In a book the third column is also a margin. Often, designers of printed and web-based pages divide the page into more columns. The illustration below shows a magazine.

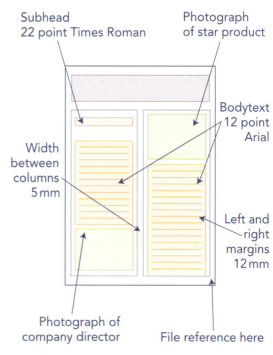

Magazine page layout

Whether it is a web page or a printed document that is being designed, the designer will need to think about the overall layout and how many columns to use.

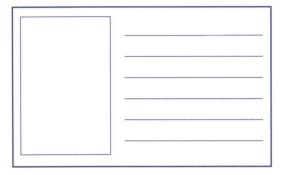

This two-column layout has an extra-wide space on the left. This can be used for hanging indents, which are helpful for scanning dense text in the right-hand column. A frame of static information, such as a table of contents for the pages on the right, can also be included in the left-hand column.

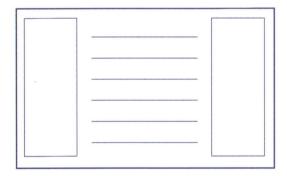

This three-column layout is often use for notes, images, even web frames. The middle column is centred and its size can be increased or decreased as needed.

A page can have one or more narrow columns (handy for notes and captions), and these columns and margins don't have to be the same width all the way around the page.

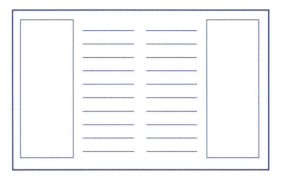

Four-column layouts are often used in newspapers and magazines. This layout is quite complex and can combine the features of two- and three-column layouts.

When any designer starts designing a document or website, he or she does not expect everything to look perfect all at once. The designer will combine the elements and take an objective look at them. The theatre designer will show the design to colleagues and see what they think. Other people may offer suggestions that will improve the design.

Placing pictures and other graphics

Pages that contain only closely packed text are often unattractive and off-putting to the reader. It is said that one picture can be worth a thousand words, but too many pictures will slow the download time of a website, and can be a distraction in a printed document. How many pictures to use, how large a picture to use and where to place it on the page are an important part of achieving balance.

Contrast – picture dominates; headline dominates

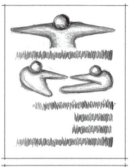
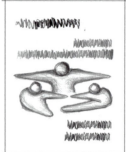

A designer's layout sketch

The theatre's designer will use only meaningful images, and would avoid using a poor quality photo or Clip Art picture just for the sake of breaking up the page with artwork. Ideally, every image in a design should be meaningful and attractive enough to be worth emphasising by surrounding it with lots of white space, or drawing attention to it in some other way. However, a designer should be careful not to clutter up pages with extra rules, boxes and screens when they are not needed for readability. These elements can help – or they can get in the way.

Obviously, designing magazine pages or a flyer for a new theatre production or an advertisement produced on a single page or on a website involves different design considerations. The designer should have a reason for every design decision made. Whether it's adding a photo, choosing column widths or setting type in an unusual face, each change that is made to a design should contribute to that design. By the time the design is completed, it should show evidence of planning and thought.

Designers often use sketches to explore different layout ideas.

The layout used will depend upon the document being produced:

- Posters advertising a theatre production, designed to attract attention from three metres away or more, need to be set in a larger, more attention-getting layout than books that will be held in the reader's hand, or than web pages.

- Advertisements in magazines and newspapers may need white space and strong borders to identify them from adjacent advertisements.

- Books require margins to accommodate the reader's thumbs without obscuring text.

- Newsletters require different designs depending on how they will be distributed, for example folded and inserted in envelopes, or if address labels are going to be placed on the back cover.

The design should be consistent throughout a document. The use of master pages and style sheets should help to ensure this.

Contrast

Of all design rules, contrast is one of the most important. Contrast creates interest in the website or document by providing variety in the design. This is similar to speech where people will use an expressive voice to emphasise a word or phrase by raising or lowering the tone, or by increasing or decreasing their speed of speech. These changes in speed and tone add expression and life to the words spoken.

Emphasize with type
EMPHASIZE with type
emphasize with type
emphasize with type
EMPHASIZE with type
emphasize with type
emphasize with type

Contrast can be added to the design by changing font types, sizes, shapes, position, weights and colours.

Using type

We have seen that type can be laid out in different ways, using margins and other graphic elements. The placing of graphics and text on a page helps to make the text readable and to communicate meaning.

However, designers also need to explore changes brought about by changing certain groups of letters or words. A common way to create emphasis is to use letters of different sizes or weights.

In longer texts, this is often achieved by using italics. In past centuries, designers often used decorative initial capitals, usually several times the height of other capitals, to call attention to the beginning of a chapter or paragraph. Today, it is common for letter initials to have different sizes, colours, styles and characters.

Designers take great care in their use of fonts – choosing the right one will help the reader to make sense of the message being communicated on a web page or in a publication. There is a wide variety of fonts to choose from. It is important that the font(s) chosen work well with the other aspects of the design. A good design will include only a limited number of fonts as too many fonts can make the design look bitty. It is better to use just one or two fonts and create variety by using different type sizes, bold, italics, etc. The designer must keep text styles consistent, for example avoiding using bold for emphasis on one page and italic for emphasis on the next. The different styles are a 'code' for the reader, and it is a bad idea to change the code halfway through the message.

The number of typefaces in use today runs into thousands and this can lead to difficulties in choosing the right one for a particular job. Because there are so many type designs to choose from, designers often select a general type style or classification to suit a graphic design, and then look for a particular typeface within the classification. There are more than 32 unique type classifications.

Typefaces can be described in a number of ways, two of the main categories being serif and sans serif.

Serif

Serif describes characters that have a line crossing the end of a stroke. This style of typeface, said to have been invented by the Romans, is also commonly referred to as 'Roman'. It is the one most often used and also one of the most legible styles. The style is familiar to all readers and is used in most reading material, including this book (see page 1).

Sans serif

Though the first sans serif (from the French word 'sans' meaning without) typeface appeared in 1816, another hundred years passed before designers began creating sans serif typefaces.

Sans serif typefaces are often used in publicity and advertising because of the large variety of styles available. The thickness and weight of the letters varies little so they are simple and neat to look at. This book also uses sans serif type (see page 68–9).

Most commonly used typefaces consist of four fonts – normal, italic, bold and extra bold. These are known as font families. One of the most popular sans serif font families is Helvetica which has more than 50 variations.

Helvetica
Helvetica Italic
Helvetica Bold
Helvetica Bold Italic
Helvetica Narrow
Helvetica Narrow Italic
Helvetica Narrow Bold
Helvetica Narrow Bold Italic
Helvetica Black
Helvetica Black Italic

The careful use of font families within a design can add visual interest and provide the reader with visual guides, for example to items of importance.

A cover using simple text and black-and-white contrast

Contrast in documents can be achieved by varying the type styles. However, too many changes can lead to a confusing design that does not put across its message.

Italic

The upper and lower case Roman alphabet was first used in a normal italic and bold family style. Today, italics can be serif or sans serif, for example:

Italic (Times New Roman)
Italic (Arial).

Italic differs from script (see page 63) in that the letters do not join together. It is usually used to emphasise text and in titles, quotes and extracts. Italic is not as legible (readable) as Roman and so is not used for large amounts of text. Lines of capitals in italic should not be used.

Script

All script faces are based on different styles of handwriting. They are usually rounded, slant to the right, and either link from letter to letter or have a tail on the letters which leads to the next. Decorative and script typefaces usually have only a single font within the family.

There are two main script fonts:

- *Formal script looks like classical pen handwriting. It is used largely for formal-type printing and invitations.*

- *Informal script looks as if it has been loosely drawn by a pen or brush. It is used for menus, advertisements, etc.*

Because script is meant to look like handwriting, there is little space between words.

Decorative

Decorative typefaces are also known as novelty faces and are used to communicate an idea, mood or theme in a display or heading, for example computer printouts, baseball bats, balloons, etc. Most decorative typefaces are designed as a single font with perhaps only a handful containing a small family such as normal, bold and outline.

Kerning

Most computer screens use fixed-pitch type, where all letters are the same width. Most books and newspapers are set in proportional-pitch type, where characters have different widths. Kerning is the term used for the adjustment of space between certain combinations of letters in proportional-pitch type before printing. It is used in desktop publishing to make the finished, printed document look better. For example, if the combination of letters 'To' is typeset with the same letter spacing as 'Th', the letters seem to be too widely spaced. Kerning is used to make the top of the letter 'T' slightly overhang the letter 'o', which gives a better effect.

Contrast in position

Sometimes designs (formal or informal) can be placed on a slant. Since we normally expect to see type in a horizontal position, placing it at an angle can be very effective. However, a tilted design should be avoided if it makes the text difficult to read comfortably.

Another method is to position the design elements of the page in such a way as to obtain contrast from the white space that surrounds all of these elements.

Contrast in shape

Trying to put a square peg into a round hole is an impossible task because the shapes are *in contrast* with each other. This idea can be used in design where the visual elements are deliberately arranged to be in conflict with each other, for example using graphics that are out of proportion to the page, using a very large display face that appears to dominate the body text or the page itself or the illustrations, using an eye-catching border or thick rule within the design.

A tilted design

Contrast in colour

A colour wheel

A good designer will use colour to create an effective looking design, including contrasting colours such as opposite colours or a colour that harmonizes, or goes with the background. The range of colour contrasts should not be limited to the natural colours – red, blue, purple, green, yellow, etc.

Colour contrast should also be considered in relation to the colour of the font, that is the amount of blackness that hits the eye. Careful selection of font, both size and weight, will give a distinctive visual colour to the overall design.

A designer needs to use contrast very carefully, because, if it makes the layout too forceful, it might send the wrong message about a product or idea.

● Designing and placing pictures

A theatre programme will usually include pictures of the actors. These will need to be in digital format. Digital images are produced by drawing or scanning pictures or by using a digital camera.

Digital cameras

A digital camera takes photographs in the same way as a traditional camera, except that it does not use light sensitive film. The digital camera has a memory in which images are stored, and extra **memory cards** can be inserted to increase the camera's storage capacity. The more memory the camera has, the more pictures can be taken before it is necessary to **download** the images on to a computer. On most digital cameras, the user can see the picture that has just been taken on a small screen at the back and, if the image is not suitable, can delete it straight away.

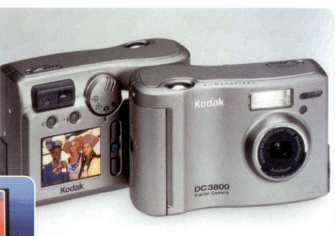

A digital camera and removable compact flash memory card

Graphics digitisers

A graphics digitiser, or **tablet**, is a board with a surface that resembles electronic tracing paper. Like paper, it is available in a range of sizes from A4 to a very large A1 size that would cover most of an office desk. A cursor, or puck, is used on a graphics digitiser to trace over a technical drawing. As the cursor is moved, pressure on the surface is detected and data about position (x and y co-ordinates) is sent to the computer using computer-aided design software such as AutoCAD.

At the moment, most users consider a graphics digitiser to be the best method of laying out pages and allowing freehand drawings to be entered into the computer. The tablet is also good for sketches and drawings. The theatre could use a tablet to add a range of hand-drawn effects to their programmes.

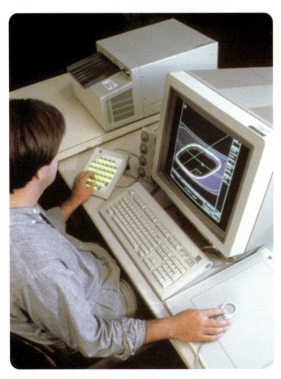

A designer uses a graphics digitiser

● Designing for publication

Before you start to lay out a page, you need to decide on paper orientation – landscape or portrait, size and how the page is to be folded if it is a leaflet.

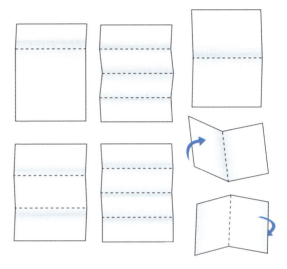

Page folds

Columns

Desktop publishing packages allow you to work in columns like those on a newspaper. Newsletters and newspapers usually use several columns on each page. This is to enable the user to scan through the document and find topics of interest. If you are designing advertising material, you will want it to have an instant impact on the reader.

Columns are less effective on posters and publicity material where the reader will probably not spend a long time reading.

Designing the page layout

You will need to decide exactly where text and pictures are to be placed. The front of the leaflet is likely to be short and simple. Its aim will be to attract the reader. Designers divide the page into a **grid** – also known as a **page template** – to help them balance text, pictures and white space (see pages 56–9). Designers say that white space is just as important as any pictures and written material when it comes to creating an impression. Plans are usually sketched out on paper before being transferred to the computer.

To understand more about page design, you also need to know about printing techniques. When leaflets are produced in very large numbers, they are printed by an offset litho method. A full-colour leaflet has to be printed four times – one print for each of three primary print colours or inks (cyan, magenta and yellow) and one for black.

A user such as a theatre can save money by printing a lot of leaflets at once, rather than printing a small quantity as and when it needs them. Another way to make savings is to print only one side of the leaflet in full colour. By using different textures and tones, it is possible to produce an effective leaflet with less than three primary print colours.

House style

The theatre, like any organisation, will want its customers to recognise its publications. This can be achieved by following a house style. A house style ensures that all leaflets and posters use a similar layout and will be instantly recognisable. Creating a house style involves developing style sheets. These contain page layout and text information including typeface and size. House style is also achieved by using set colours.

You can easily research house styles by looking at the labels on supermarket own-brand goods.

Importing text and images

Desktop publishing packages are designed to allow you to import images and text from other packages. It is likely that the text will have been prepared on a word processor. Most word processors contain a wide range of facilities such as a thesaurus and grammar and spell checkers that are more sophisticated than those contained within DTP packages. This is because they are designed primarily to work with text.

Similarly, graphics are usually manipulated in other packages before being placed on to the DTP page grid.

Unfortunately, different packages such as word processing and graphics packages save files in a range of different formats. Partly, this is because different manufacturers pick different ways of compressing files. There are also copyright issues as programmers often take out patents on their inventions. Most DTP packages accept a wide range of formats to enable you to import elements on to your page.

Below are the most common formats for each application.

Graphics files

- gif (bitmapped colour graphic file format)
- jpeg (joint photographic expert group)
- pict (apple mac standard)
- tiff (tagged image format)
- eps (encapsulated postscript)
- bmp (bitmap file)
- pcx (pc paintbrush file)
- pcd (photo cd)

Text files

- doc (word file)
- rtf (rich text format)
- txt (plain text file)

Special effects

Desktop publishing packages offer special effects such as **text wrapping** which allows you to make text flow around a graphic. Packages usually include drop shadows, overlays and a wide variety of other facilities.

Printing

When producing a leaflet in full colour, you should first print it out on a colour printer to see how effective it is. This will allow you to make adjustments.

For *professional* printing purposes, the leaflet will be printed using **colour separation**. This involves separating the page into the three primary printing colours (cyan, magenta and yellow) plus black. Most desktop publishing packages do this automatically.

Desktop publishing programs can be used to produce business forms, application forms, annual reports, business proposals, catalogues, menus, product lists, brochures, flyers, posters, logos, letterheads, marketing materials, advertisements, newsletters, newspapers and magazines, packaging, book jackets, CD inserts, manuals, books and so on.

Preparing the pictures – using graphics software

Before you insert pictures into your DTP page grid, they will usually need to be manipulated in a graphics application package. You can use programs such as Photoshop, Corel and Paint to manipulate images.

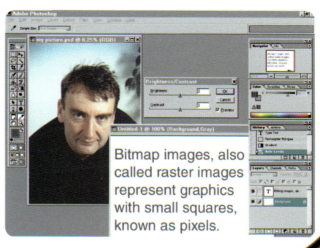

Bitmap images, also called raster images represent graphics with small squares, known as pixels.

A graphics package

Graphics applications packages can be divided into four main types, according to their function:

- graphs and charts, sometimes called business graphics, programs

- painting and drawing programs

- image manipulation programs

- computer-aided design (CAD) packages.

Graphics files are of two main types:

- **vector graphics**

- **bitmaps**.

Most graphics programs offer good facilities for freehand drawing, with a wide choice of pens, brushes and drawing styles, and a wide range of colours and patterns.

The artist can use a range of standard shapes. These shapes can be filled with colour selected from the pallet. Shapes and other elements can be rotated and flipped vertically or horizontally. Choices are made mainly with a mouse and icons. Areas to be deleted, copied or moved can be selected with the mouse. There is also usually a zoom facility to change individual pixels.

Vector graphics

With vector graphics, lines are stored in the computer as equations. They are expressed in vector format so they have a starting point, a length and a direction. Vector graphics are easy to change without any loss of resolution. When a vector graphics image is enlarged, the number of pixels used to make up the image increases in proportion, so the detail remains the same.

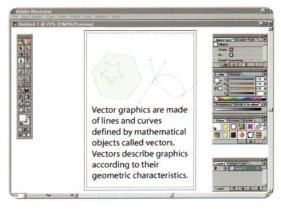

Vector graphic

As well as being used in painting and drawing applications software, vector graphics are used in CAD packages.

The theatre logo will have been designed in a vector graphics package.

Bitmap graphics

Bitmap graphics are used in software designed to manipulate images. Such software is often used alongside a digital camera and can change and enhance pictures that have been taken. A bitmap file represents each pixel on the screen as a single **bit** of information. If the pixel is in colour, additional bits will need to be stored. If the user wants to change a bitmapped image, the software has to alter it one pixel at a time. If the image is enlarged, the number of pixels stays the same and, as a result, the pixels move apart, making the image look grainy and less clear.

Bitmap graphic

Importing from other packages

Most graphics applications programs will import sets of data from a database or spreadsheet.

Some offer a choice of graphs including pie charts, bar charts, line graphs and x-y or scatter graphs that can be labelled in terms of both the axes and the data, as appropriate. They offer a range of colours and formats to enhance the presentation of graphs and charts.

Most drawing programs offer good facilities for freehand drawing, with a wide choice of pens, brushes and drawing styles, and a wide range of colours and patterns. They also offer a range of standard shapes including pictures.

Choices are made mainly with a mouse and icons, and a zoom facility allows you to change individual pixels. Areas can be deleted, copied, resized and moved.

You can use painting and drawing applications software to produce:

- pictures on the screen, providing a chance to be creative – the pictures can be printed
- simple illustrations for use on documents.

Activity:

Explore the use of DTP in the production of a theatre programme.

Clip Art

Clip Art are illustrations that are copyright-free and intended for use in documents of all kinds, where the user does not want to draw something from scratch. Clip Art illustrations can be added to all kinds of documents, from word processed documents, spreadsheets, desktop published documents to graphics. The use of Clip Art can save time and help to produce a document with a more professional appearance. Disks containing Clip Art can be bought separately or as part of a DTP or graphics package. As many as one million images may be available in a Clip Art package.

● Other types of theatre revenue

Souvenirs

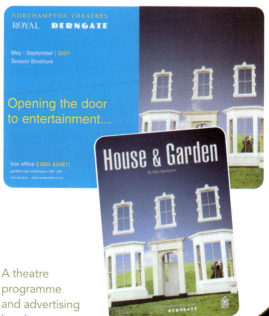

A theatre programme and advertising brochure

Theatre books and postcards, CDs, T-shirts and a wide range of other souvenir items are often used as additional sources of income for a theatre. Many of them are produced using ICT, ranging from DTP and graphics packages to computer-aided design and manufacture (CADCAM).

Activity:

Explore ways in which ICT systems can be used to produce one souvenir item for use in a theatre.

Catering

Most theatres try to help customers relax and enjoy themselves. They offer seating areas with bars and snack facilities, and some even have games areas. Many theatres have automatic vending machines selling drinks and snacks. Some of the latest vending machines use ICT to automatically send data on sales and stock levels (how many products are stored in the machine) to the maintenance engineer.

Activity:

Explore the use of automatic vending machines.

Industrial sponsorship

Industrial sponsorship, particularly for the performing arts, is a vital part of revenue. While many big sponsors may prefer to be associated with the more glamorous types of traditional theatre, theatre managers are always wise to look to local companies for support, particularly where there is a link between something or someone in a play, and the local area.

The search for industrial sponsorship involves keeping up-to-date records of local companies and using mail merge facilities to write to them. It is essential for the theatre to show targeted companies how sponsorship can benefit them. Video and presentation software – sometimes called business graphics software – are often used to do this.

Activity:

Design a database and mail merge facility for use in a theatre.

Presentation software

Business graphics presentation software can be used:

- to present statistics in a form that can be easily understood, for example using a pie chart to show the different age groups of population in a town, or using a line graph to show how the price of petrol has increased over a number of years

- to sketch mathematical functions.

Presentation software can put together text and pictures in a similar way to a DTP program. The end result is usually a set of high quality slides, which can have some animation (movement), to be used in a presentation to an audience. The presentation is made via a computer screen, or for better effect, on a large screen using a projector.

Presentation software does not usually need to produce documents in as high a resolution as DTP software. The quality of this type of presentation can have a very positive effect on the image of the theatre using it. It can help to explain information that can be technical and complicated in an easily understandable way.

A document produced by a presentation program is usually divided into slides. The software offers word processing features, with a good range of fonts and other format options. Lines, boxes, bullets, borders and colour can be used to enhance effect. Style sheets can be used to help make main text, headings and subheadings consistent. The master page and paragraph styles for a document can be saved as a template to ensure that each page or slide looks the same overall.

Presentation software usually has a drawing facility. It can import word processing and other files. It can also import data from scanners and digital cameras and utilise this. The software has good facilities for arranging text and pictures together in eye-catching ways, and changing their sizes. Pictures can also be **cropped** – cutting off and discarding part of a picture that is not needed.

Typical applications of presentation software are:

- to launch new products
- to give a keynote address to an audience
- to raise funds for the theatre.

Activity:

Design a presentation to be given to a local company to raise funds for a theatre production.

Getting an audience

Attracting an audience is one of the most important aspects of running a theatre. The first stage is to identify the type of person who may want to attend a production. The next stage involves:

- advertising – telling the potential audience what the show is, what it is about and getting them to want to see it
- motivating customers – encouraging them to buy tickets
- selling the tickets.

Each stage can involve the use of new technology.

Advertising

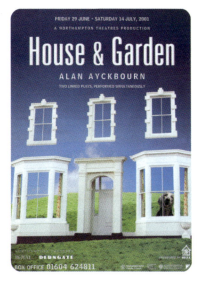

A poster for a theatre production. The graphics are designed to match the programme and publicity materials

There are various ways to advertise a production. These include advertisements in newspapers and magazines, on posters, television and radio, in free leaflets, on badges and stickers, and direct marketing (sending out letters and leaflets) to individuals who have attended the theatre's productions in the past. It is very important that all the different forms of advertising follow a consistent house style (see page 66). If direct marketing is to be used, the theatre management first needs to build a database of customers.

The Internet offers another opportunity to advertise, either by sending e-mails to individual customers, or through the use of websites.

Activity:

Design a customer database for use in a theatre.

Activity:

Design a system to promote theatre productions through printed material.

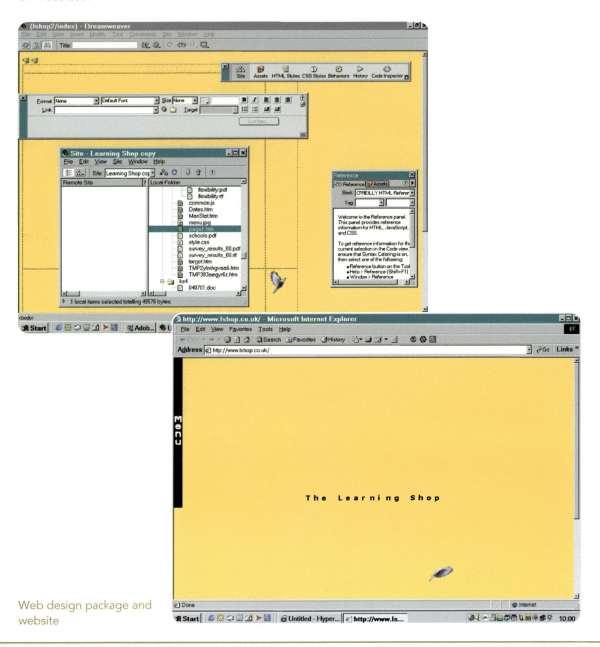

Web design package and website

Using the Internet – websites

Websites can be professionally designed and created, or they can be designed and created by individuals working in a theatre setting. A number of software packages can be used to design and create websites.

All organisations, from shops to schools, can benefit from a website. A website aids communication between the organisation and its customers. It can be used to tell people about the organisation, its products and services. A theatre can design its website so that customers are able to make electronic bookings. Websites can be designed to be accessed through computers, televisions and mobile phones.

What is a website?

A website is a group of related pages. All websites have a **home page** to act as a starting point for accessing the rest of the pages. Unlike paper, a web page can be of any length and size. It has nothing to do with the size of a printed piece of paper.

A web page may include any or all of the following:

- Formatted text – headings, bold, italic, indented lists and a number of other kinds of formatting to make texts easier and more interesting to read.

- Graphics and multimedia – images, colours, patterns, quicktime movies, Java applets, graphics and multimedia, including sounds.

- Hyperlinks – these may link to other pages or websites, download files and open e-mail forms.

- Forms – including edit boxes, radio buttons, check boxes and pop-up menus.

- Tables – to display text and graphics and produce a neat appearance.

- Frames – split the browser window into sub-windows allowing more than one web page to be shown at any time.

Web pages and sites are viewed through **web browsers**. There are a number of different browsers on the market. These browsers run on different platforms, for example PC, Macintosh, WAP (for mobile phones). The version of the browser that you use will depend on the age and capability of your computer. When you design a site, you must bear this in mind. Also, it is advisable to use standard fonts, etc., so that the majority of users will be able to read the site in full.

HTML

Websites are always written in **HTML (hypertext mark-up language)**. You can design a site completely in HTML but it is simpler to use a website design package. A web design program usually helps the user to construct HTML code.

HTML is constantly being developed and sometimes new versions of the code will not work with the software you are using. Unfortunately, not all web browsers interpret HTML codes in the same way. Not all web browsers support all versions of HTML code. For this reason, it is worth checking your website in a number of browsers to see what it looks like.

The types of software you could use to create a website include: Adobe PageMill, Microsoft FrontPage, Dream Weaver, Hot Dog. Remember also that computer screens can be set to different resolutions. When you change the resolution of a computer screen, you change the size of all objects and text on it. If you design a page using a high resolution screen, it will appear larger when viewed on a low resolution screen.

WAP phones

Manufacturers of mobile phone handsets such as Nokia, Ericsson and Motorola are investing heavily in mobile phone design and technology to allow handsets to display HTML pages. The latest WAP phones use Wireless Mark-up Language. The link between the handset and the web server is managed by the Wireless Application Protocol (WAP), which is the wireless equivalent of the HTTP server **protocol**.

Activity:

Explain what is meant by protocol.

Planning your website

To produce an effective website takes careful planning. Before you start, you should ask yourself the following questions:

- What do I want my pages to look like? If you plan a number of pages, you may want to use consistent formatting, colours, patterns, logos and other features to give your site its own identity.

- Are my pages going to be long or short? Long pages make it possible to provide more information but are slow to load and can be annoying to the end user who has to keep on scrolling to find information. They can also prove difficult to print. Short pages load quickly but can provide less information.

- Will my pages rely heavily on graphics? Remember that some browsers will not read graphics and not all visitors to your site will be willing to wait while graphic images load and appear on the screen.

- How do I want to organise my site? Think carefully about how end users will **navigate** (move around) your site and how they will know where they are.

Working with hyperlinks

Hyperlinks are one of the most important aspects of a website. They allow the user to move to another website or page simply by clicking on the link. There are two main kinds of documents when working with links:

- The **source document** is the document that contains a link.

- The **destination** or **referenced document** is the one displayed when you click on a link.

To set up a link on a web page, you need to insert the address of the destination document – this is known as its **Uniform Resource Locator (URL)**.

The URL is where the document is to be found on the Internet – its reference.

It is very similar to the path name that you have on every file on your hard disk. The difference is that rather than all the files being stored on a single hard disk, they are stored on hard disks all over the world.

You can often recognise linked text or a linked graphic on a web page by the coloured underline or border around it. You can change these colours using the **inspector**.

There are two types of URL:

- An **absolute reference** always includes the entire path name of the referenced location, for example: http://www.lshop.co.uk

- A **relative reference** is usually a URL for a document in the same directory as the current document. A relative reference gives only information about where the file is located, starting from the address of the file that is open. It includes the path name to the reference location relative to the source document. For example, a relative reference for a document in the same directory as the file index.html could be: catalogue.html

You must include absolute references to any location outside your own website.

Remember that relative references will not work if you move your pages from one directory to another, or from one server to another.

Although URLs are the most common references used in web pages, there are other address types:

- http:// opens a web page.

- file:// opens a file.

- ftp:// connects to an ftp server to download files.

- telnet:// connects to a server via telnet.

- gopher:// connects to a gopher service.

- mailto: sends an e-mail message.

- news: opens a Usenet newsgroup.

● Connecting to the Internet

To be able to connect to the Internet, the computer you are using will require a device called a **modem**. A modem is said to be **dialling-up** when it connects to the Internet. In the same way, files sent to the Internet are **uploaded**, while files taken from the Internet are **downloaded**. Because of the costs involved, the data transmission speed of a modem is particularly important when accessing the Internet.

Software is also needed to make a connection to the Internet. Standards, or protocols, have been developed in order to improve speed and reliability of data transfer over the Internet.

Protocols

In order to connect to the Internet, you will need a protocol called **TCP/IP (Transmission Control Protocol/Internet Protocol)**. This protocol is set up as part of the system software running on the computer. The function of the TCP is to break up data into manageable chunks or **packets** that bear the address they are being sent to.

The IP routes the packets from machine to machine, and the TCP then puts data back together in the correct order so that it can be used.

These functions are very important because of the way the Internet works. If you are sending a message from the UK to the United States, for example, the first packet of data may be sent via France and Sweden, while the second packet could travel via a satellite link to Australia and on. The route does not matter as TCP/IP will make sure that the packets arrive in the correct place and are reassembled in the correct order, even if the first packet arrives last.

The protocol requires that every computer linked to the TCP/IP network should have a unique **IP (Internet Protocol)** address. The address can be just numeric, composed of four sets of numbers, each between 0 and 255, separated by dots. An example would be: 195.107.24.242. If you want to allow other users on the web to access your computer you must have a fixed IP address.

IP address numbers are allocated by **internet service providers (ISPs)** who make sure that the same number is not given out twice. Because IP address numbers are unique, it means that any computer on the Internet can be recognised, no matter where it is located. An IP number can have a name attached to it to give the address more meaning.

An additional piece of software is needed wherever the connection to the Internet is made through a modem and ISP. The software will enable the modem to dial-up the telephone number to reach the service provider, and will allow TCP/IP to operate on the computer.

Motivating customers

Everyone loves a bargain. Providing discounts for individuals such as regular theatre-goers or those who book early, for parties, and special subscription rates, is a vital part of encouraging people to buy tickets. A theatre may even give away complimentary tickets to ensure a full house. Once the theatre management has decided upon the different prices of seats, an ICT system needs to be developed that is easy to operate but which ensures that any special offers are in line with requirements. For example, if a 10 per cent reduction is given to someone booking three performances, the system needs to check they are booking all three performances before giving the discount.

Activity:

Design a simple user interface for a ticket-issuing system that includes special offers.

Selling tickets

Once a person has decided to buy a ticket, the theatre needs to make this process as easy as possible. Many years ago, people needed to visit the theatre and pay with cash at the box office. Today, people expect to use credit cards, telephone booking, agencies and the Internet.

Activity:

Design an Internet-based booking system for a theatre.

New forms of entertainment

ICT has led to the development of a wide range of new forms of entertainment. Even existing forms of entertainment are changing. The cinema used to be confined to reels of acetate film with the musical score, or **sound track**, recorded on to the film's edge. Home entertainment was restricted to lower quality video. Today, digital recording technology has revolutionised the cinema and the quality we can achieve in our homes using **DVD** (see page 26) and other new digital technologies such as CDs and **mini disks**.

It is possible to broadcast hundreds of entertainment channels through the Internet and digital television.

Computer games have also been made possible by new digital technologies. It is now possible to simulate real adventure situations, and **virtual reality** systems are likely to extend this still further.

These changes have occurred due to the advance in functions such as video editing, animation and **digital sound**.

Editing moving pictures – video digitisers

ICT can be used to edit moving pictures in a similar way to editing still pictures.

A **video digitiser** is used to convert a video picture into a computer image. A video camera is used to produce a picture. The digitiser, a combination of hardware and software, converts the analogue

(see page 115) video signal into a digital signal in the computer's memory. Each frame from a video is converted so that it can be played back or printed in any required **sequence**. The stored image can be used in the same way as any other graphic.

Video digitising is used to capture a **frame** from a video sequence so that it can be printed in a document or magazine, and in making television adverts and pop music videos.

Once a digital video signal has been captured, it can be manipulated and changed, and special effects can be added. There are a number of software programs now available for home and commercial use. Moving pictures require a large amount of memory. The development of DVDs has enabled the storage of over 4.7 gigabytes of digital information on a single disk. Larger capacity disks are being developed all the time.

Moving images are usually stored on DVDs in a format called **DVI (digital video interface)**.

Activity:

Produce a short video sequence advertising your local area.

Authoring software

Software that pulls together animation (cartoons and puppetry), sound and video is called **authoring software**. It enables the designer to put together various elements in the same way as a theatre director puts together a stage production.

Help sheet 4: multimedia publishing

The message (1) and image (2) phase are where the scope of the project is identified and plans are made accordingly.

1 Message (decide on content)

- What do you want to say?
- Identify audience – who will use your system?
- Identify context – where and how will your system be viewed?
- List key points.

2 Image (decide on overall look of finished document)

- Look at other examples.
- Identify the *scope* of the project.
- Compose text.
- Storyboard mock-ups of bits and pieces:
  - screen layout (grid)
  - thumbnail sketches of text and image treatments
  - navigation interface
  - flowchart of possible sequences
  - thumbnail of buttons and icons.
- Research sources of existing graphics and media.
- Extent of media use.
- Any digital video?
- Any digital audio?

3 Choose hardware and software

Only prototypes of the product are produced in this phase. Once you create anything that will be used in the final product, you are in the production phase.

- Select possible hardware platform/software packages for delivery.
- Define user environment/hardware limitations.
- Determine output requirements (screen, web, monitor).

4 Production

You should start to make your system only once you have identified the exact content and goals of the project.

- Create interface with place-holders for graphics, text, and other media.
- Usability test (user response).
- Create/import graphic elements.
- Create, import, size, modify: graphics, sound, animations.
- Create, rephrase text.
- Usability test (user response).
- Digitise video, audio, still-frames.
- Assemble all elements into interface.

5 Evaluation (does it work?)

- Usability test.
- 'Debug' session.
- Evaluate content or structure to see if it works or requires modification.
- Revise (at whatever level necessary).

Animation

Authoring software and animation have brought about a revival in cartoons and puppetry. A large number of today's pop videos bring together puppetry, animation and real film. The first major film to be based on this new technology was *Who Framed Roger Rabbit?*

There are a number of specialist puppetry and animation companies producing animations such as *Morph*, *Wallace and Grommit*, *Chicken Run*, *Toy Story* and *Bill and Ben*.

The Internet also contains many sites on puppetry and animation.

Moving images are actually fixed images redrawn many times per second. This means that even a few seconds of moving video can take up as much storage space as dozens or hundreds of still pictures. For this reason, data is usually stored on CD-ROMs or DVDs. As access to the pictures needs to be fast if the animation is to run effectively, CD-ROM access speeds and times become very important. Each picture in an animation is known as a frame.

Activity:

Design a short animation for a computer game or children's cartoon.

Another important factor is the size of the picture files and the amount of redrawing that has to occur in each frame. Computer game animators reduce the picture size by fixing a common background and changing only small objects against this background in each **frame**.

There is a wide range of software available for creating animations, particularly for use on the Internet. All of the programs work in a similar way, mainly by using **layers**. Layers are like a stack of acetate sheets or panes of glass. Each item in the animation is stored on a different layer. This enables the animator to create an individual snapshot of movement for each object in the animation. The first position is created and recorded, the next frame in the sequence is then created by moving or changing the object until the complete animation sequence for that layer is achieved.

Frames and layers from a simple animation

Most animation programs have a number of tools to help the designer. One of the most important tools is the **between** or **'tween'** tool. This allows an object to be drawn on the first frame and the last frame and then automatically generates the position or shape of the object on all of the frames between the first and last frame. This tool, sometimes also called a **morphing** tool, saves hours of drawing.

Some packages will even allow you to mark out a path that you want an object to move through and will then generate the necessary movement.

Animation packages are available to enable design in both two and three dimensions (2D/3D). The easiest packages to use are those that generate 2D animation. The 3D packages use **wire frame** objects in a similar way to 3D computer-aided design packages. When colour and texture are added to 3D animations (rendering), the images are very large.

Systems used for 3D animation need a large amount of computing power.

● Adding sound

Sound can be added to animations, pictures, video and information systems. Computers are built to recognise different sounds. Computers usually come with built-in speakers and basic sound capability, but to achieve the best results, they need peripheral devices such as loudspeakers, microphones and a sound card.

Microphone and speech recognition software

A microphone is used as the input device for a speech recognition system. Apart from speech, a microphone can record music or any other kind of sound that can be transmitted to the computer's memory. (See also 'Microphones and speech recognition software' on pages 18–19.)

Storing sounds

Sounds are stored in a number of different digital formats depending on the software. The volume of sound is also stored in digital format. To achieve this, when we record sound using a microphone, the analogue signal (continuous variation between low and high pitch) needs to be converted into a **digital value** (a pitch with distinct steps rather than a smooth scale). Windows uses **WAV** (short for wave) files. WAV files contain a digital representation of sound waves.

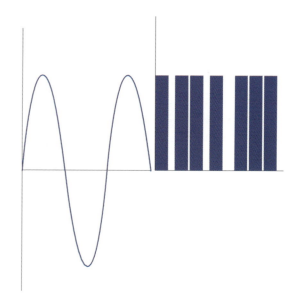

Analogue and digital sound signals

The quality and accuracy of a sound file depends upon the **sampling rate**. The higher the sampling rate, the greater the accuracy, but the larger the file. It is best to think of sampling rates in a similar way to the resolution of a graphics image. The more dots or pixels in the image, the better its quality. Similarly, the more samples that are taken of a sound, the better its quality.

Activity:

Design a sound system and sequence for a short animation.

Sound is output through the speaker system. The difficulty with sampling sounds using a microphone is that it will also pick up all of the background noise. The best sampled sounds are captured using a **musical instrument digital interface (MIDI)**. A MIDI uses hardware and software to connect an electronic musical instrument such as a keyboard, synthesiser or drum machine to a computer. The frequency, pitch and other musical data received is converted to digital data which can be read by the computer. Music played on the instrument can be stored on the computer, which can, in turn, send signals back to the instrument.

MIDI files are recorded more like musical scores than the digital files recorded in WAV files. The MIDI file represents notes and instruments. The computer has to play these notes in a similar way to a musician. Because of this, MIDI files are much smaller than WAV files and can contain a higher resolution sound file.

MIDI systems are also used to control specialised devices such as theatrical lighting.

Mixing and sequencing

An organised series of MIDI commands is called a sequence. Sequencing is the name given to the process of deciding in what order to play a sound. As with animation, each sound is saved as a different layer, called a **track**.

This enables a single track to be manipulated without affecting the other tracks.

You can also distort, stretch, repeat and alter the pitch and volume of a track, or you may decide not to play a particular track continuously.

Each track will have its own sequence. Once all of the sequences are complete, you will be able to play the whole composition together. Composers will often spend hours getting each track right before they are happy with the combined sound. To save space, the separate tracks can then be combined on to a single track.

A sound sequence showing tracks

● Cinema

Cinemas and theatres have many things in common including their use of ICT. A modern cinema uses ICT and traditional non-IT solutions for a wide number of tasks including:

● ticket-booking systems

● Internet site

● staff rotas

● promotion materials

- online ticket systems
- cash flow
- automatic lighting systems
- central management system
- accounts
- scheduling
- user interfaces
- alarms.

Unlike theatres which are usually independent or parts of small chains, most cinemas are parts of large chains of multiplex cinemas, sometimes owned by the companies which make the films they show. Films are usually purchased for the whole chain and shown in cinemas around the country. Where theatres have just one show on at a time, cinemas have a number of films to schedule. This was not always the case. Early cinemas had only a single screen. It is common today for each multiplex cinema to have between six and nine screens, each one in a separate theatre. Multiplexes with nine theatres can often hold up to 2000 paying customers. The smallest theatres in a multiplex usually hold about 150 paying customers. Each theatre usually also has areas where people in wheelchairs can sit.

With so many different films showing, all of which start at different times and have a different running time, the booking systems used in a modern multiplex cinemas rely upon ICT to manage ticket issuing. The problem of ticket issuing is made more complex by a range of different prices based upon film, time of the day and type of customer, for example child and disabled people discounts.

Activity:

Design a booking system for use at a cinema cash desk. Your system should ensure that the number of customers does not exceed the number of seats for any one screen. It should be easily amended for different films each week.

Modern cinemas accept bookings over the phone, by Internet and in person. Telephone bookings cost an additional 25p per booking to cover administration costs. Cinemas usually accept cash, cheques, credit card and debit card payments. This means that ICT systems at cinema cash desks must be able to cope with all these different forms of payment.

To attract regular visitors, some cinemas offer monthly season tickets. Season ticket holders have to book their seat each time they go, but they show their season ticket to the cashier as payment.

Activity:

Design an automatic staff rota system to ensure the cinema is fully staffed on a weekly basis. Your system should print out a weekly rota list to be posted on the staff noticeboard.

The monthly season ticket approach has enabled cinemas to build a database of regular customers and obtain addresses. This enables them to supplement on-screen advertisements with mailings of leaflets.

Activity:

Design a mail merge system for the distribution of cinema leaflets.

Activity:

Design a full-page advertisement for a cinema. Your advertisement should be web-based, attractive and easy to update as films and timings change.

Activity:

Design a set of document templates to be used by the business administration centre of a cinema. These should include sample letters to successful and unsuccessful job applicants, letters of dismissal, contracts of employment and staff information sheets.

Nowadays, almost everything in a modern cinema is digitally controlled, including the fire alarms, smoke detectors, sprinklers, lights and exit doors.

Most cinemas do not allow smoking, but there is still a risk of fire. A cinema needs to be able to evacuate people rapidly in the event of a fire. In order to do this, cinemas have clearly marked exit doors. The exit doors have push bars and sometimes people let their friends into the cinema without paying. To prevent this, alarms are fitted on the doors.

Digital soundtracks are a key part of today's cinema experience. Films are often recorded digitally to ensure high quality resolution and transfer to DVD and video.

Use of ICT in the entertainment industry

Use of ICT in the banking and finance sector

Until recently, the only access people had to banking services was to visit their high street branch. The introduction of ICT to banking has led to a range of ways in which people can 'visit' their bank, including using the phone and the Internet.

Bank branches of the future

A bank branch of tomorrow

Today's high street bank branch, with its row of cashiers and formal atmosphere, will soon be a thing of the past. ICT is changing the way banks work and how they provide services to customers.

Walk around a university campus, a modern international airport or an international railway station, and there is a good chance that you will see the bank branch of the future. Bank branches in universities are clean, smart and secure. They contain a large number of **cash machines** and **multimedia kiosks**. Multimedia kiosks make use of video, sound and text to provide an interesting interface between the bank and its customers. You can withdraw cash, deposit cheques and apply for a loan. For most of the time, no staff at all are present.

Modern electronic banks are being located wherever their customers may have an occasional few minutes of free time, including in larger supermarkets and shops.

In some modern banks, staff are free to roam, asking customers if they require assistance, while electronic terminals take care of the majority of banking functions.

Comfortable seats, coffee and tea, chilled water machines and children's play areas are all being added to create an informal atmosphere. Customers are encouraged to use **touch screens** that advertise a wide range of financial products. Other machines provide local information and even sell cinema and theatre tickets.

This approach offers considerable financial savings for a bank. The average UK high street bank employs eleven staff, not all of whom deal with customers. The average modern electronic bank branch employs fewer than six staff.

In the early days of ICT, people predicted bank branches with electronic machines that would perform every banking function, including issuing and managing mortgages, insurance and everyday cash dispensing. The bank machines themselves have been steadily falling in price as technology and communications have improved. Unfortunately, the prediction forgot one important factor. Who would want to be waiting in a queue to draw £20 cash behind a customer applying for a mortgage at the same machine?

Single-purpose terminals like the cash withdrawal machines we use today, look set to stay.

● Telephone banking

Telephone banking systems offer customers 'any time, anywhere' banking.

Call centres

A bank's call centre

Call centres are often seen by banks as a step towards low-cost banking. While they are about 50 times more expensive than a fully self-service operation on the Internet, they are much cheaper than a high street bank branch. Call centres can use operators, although fully automated systems are now being used by some banks.

For a call centre to be effective, the operator needs instant access to account details when a customer telephones. This is achieved using new telephone technology which allows people receiving a call to see who is phoning them – BT's fixed-line (land line) system is known as a caller display. The automatic transfer of telephone numbers in this way is called **caller line identification (CLI)**. Call centres use this system to identify the caller and link directly into its customer database, so when a customer phones the call centre, his or her file is automatically called up.

Activity:

Design a system that enables telephone calls to be linked to a database using a CLI system.

Of course, the 'customer' could be someone else using the real customer's phone number. To improve security, bank customers are issued with a password or can choose their own. As an added security measure, the call centre operator should not know the full password. When the customer phones the call centre, the operator asks for the customer's name and account name.

The operator calls up the customer's file, and before he or she can access the database, the program asks for two or three letters of the password. These letters are chosen at random and could be, for example, the second and fifth letters of the password. In this way, the operator does not learn the password but is able to access the database.

Activity:

Explore a system which can randomly ask for parts of a password without disclosing the whole password. If the password letters asked for are correct, your database should open a customer file.

Fully automated telephone banking systems use **interactive voice recognition (IVR)** or the telephone keypad to access and control customer accounts. These automated centres are also referred to as automated non-personal call centres.

Activity:

Explore and design a voice-activated system.

Computer telephone integration

The integration of telephone systems with computers is known as computer telephone integration (CTI). CTI is dependent upon databases containing information on customers and potential customers. Telephone operators need to be able to call up all relevant customer details, including letters, outstanding balances, savings accounts and credit status. Organisations using CTI usually issue their telephone operators with a written script to follow each time a customer phones. The telephone operator then selects a series of boxes on screen. As each box is completed, it leads to another box and the complete sequence carries out the customer's instructions.

Internet banking

Internet or online banking allows customers to manage their bank accounts from home, making visits to a bank branch unnecessary. Research shows that many business executives have not visited their bank branch for more than ten years!

It also gives customers freedom to choose banks anywhere in the world, with accounts in any currency. An example of this is the Brazilian executives who, during 1994, invested their money in foreign banks and avoided 5000 per cent inflation in Brazil. Using the Internet, customers can switch their accounts between banks and countries, and achieve the highest possible rates of interest, wherever they are offered in the world.

The first Internet bank – a 'virtual' bank – began as a joke in the USA. Its founders did not intend to set up a bank. They started an Internet company that charged users a fee to be sent a joke each day. The company soon ran into problems as there was no easy way it could charge customers. Noticing a gap in the market in October 1994, it set up the first virtual bank called First Virtual. Within eighteen months, it had over 125 000 customers in 144 countries.

The first European Internet banking took place in Denmark, where the Danes have the highest proportion of computers per household in the world.

Recent research has shown that Internet banking is used mainly by highly paid customers, who tend to be more willing to buy a variety of financial services, like share trading. As web browsing usually takes place during leisure time, banks have found the Internet to be a good place to sell these services.

Some banks, for example Barclays, have launched themselves as an ISP (Internet service provider). This provides closer links with their customers, and improves security. Some banks use the telephone to check instructions given over the Internet.

Major banks are attempting to find a balance between high street branches, telephone banking and Internet banking.

Attracting customers

To attract more Internet customers, banks are linking with popular retailers and sporting activities. An example of this is Nationwide, which believes its site is the most frequently visited financial services site in Britain, achieved by linking to its sponsorship of the Football League.

A number of large banks are negotiating deals with manufacturers of major brands to by-pass shops altogether and sell goods through the banks themselves.

Software companies are now integrating PC banking into their personal finance packages. Microsoft's Money, and Quicken are two examples of packages that do this.

The Internet market

The Internet market is vast. Almost six hundred million mobile phones, palmtops and telecommunications connections are being sold annually worldwide. One mobile phone manufacturer, Motorola, predicts that by 2009 there will be one billion fixed-line phone users, one billion mobile phone users and one billion Internet users worldwide. Some banks are considering giving customers free palmtops and PCs. In the UK, Internet access is doubling every six months. In the USA, 40 per cent of homes had Internet access in 2000.

Advantages of Internet banking

- Internet banking offers a much cheaper way to provide customer services, as no branches are needed, and customers input their own data. It costs banks as much to set up a single high street branch as it does to set up a fully functioning Internet bank. A bank transaction through a high street branch costs about 70p. The same transaction through a call centre costs about 35p, via a cash machine 19p and over the Internet less than 1p.

- Internet banking allows the banks to monitor customer use very easily. This enables them to build up personal customer profiles, and some banks vary their charges according to the services customers use. Customer profiles have proved so effective that retailers like Microsoft, Virgin, Dixon and Tesco have all moved into the banking market-place.

Loyalty card schemes gave retailers an advantage as they had already built up sophisticated databases of customers. Insurers have also moved into banking following a trend set by building societies. Some retailers and insurers have made alliances with other banks and financial institutions, for example Consignia (the Post Office) and the Co-operative Bank.

- Businesses can save 90 per cent of their buying costs by moving to electronic systems.

Disadvantages

- There is some recognition that the domination of the Internet by the English (American) language is causing negative reactions from customers in some countries.

- Police are worried at the development of major banks being set up by criminal groups.

Mobile phone banking

A number of banks have invested heavily in mobile telephone banking. Recent mobile phone technology linked to handheld **personal organisers** and palmtop computers lends itself to 'any time, anywhere' banking. Customers need never be out of touch with their banks wherever they are in the world.

From e-commerce to m-commerce

Businesses using the Internet are said to be e-businesses, short for electronic businesses. Internet trade is called e-commerce, or electronic commerce. Mobile phone technology has produced a new term – m-commerce – which means mobile commerce.

Access to the Internet using **handheld terminals**, especially mobile phones, has been growing at an astonishing rate. Text messaging (often known as SMS for Short Message Service), which allows mobile phone users to send typed messages to other mobile phone handsets, is now widely used.

Activity:

Design a banking text messaging service that makes use of mobile phone technology.

It has been possible to read **e-mails** over a handheld terminal or a mobile phone connected to a laptop for years. But speed has been a problem and the idea that a device, such as a mobile phone handset, with a small low-resolution monochrome screen, limited memory, a numeric keypad and reliant on wireless technology could be used to access the world wide web initially seemed like science fiction.

The first generation of mobile phones worked on an analogue system, but the current second generation of digital services, known as the Global System for Mobile Communications (GSM), has greatly improved the service.

A new, faster system is to be introduced called the Universal Mobile Telecommunications System (UMTS).

It used to be thought that mobile phone services would not be able to offer the bandwidth (see page 31) of a terrestrial (land-based) network. Certainly, the current bandwidth is inadequate for all but short text messages. But UMTS technology offers bandwidths which are four times faster than Integrated Services Digital Network (ISDN). General Packet Radio Service (GPRS) technology is not as fast as UMTS but will provide improved bandwidth.

So once again science fiction has become science fact, and it seems likely that there will be more mobile devices accessing the Internet than PCs. Mobile phones – for years getting smaller and smaller – are about to get bigger to allow for larger screens.

In Japan, mobile phones have been the most popular way to access the Internet for years. It will soon be possible to access the Internet, banking and experts online from mobile phones quicker than using a desktop computer.

A solution is emerging as to how these handsets could display HTML pages, based upon a version of the extensible mark-up language (XML) called Wireless Mark-up Language (WML). The link between the handset and the web server is then managed by the Wireless Application Protocol (WAP), which can be regarded as the wireless equivalent of the HTTP server protocol (see explanation of Protocol on page 75).

There is no need to have a new URL for your website on mobile phones. The WAP technology ensures that the HTTP server recognises that the call is coming

from a WAP device, and routes the request to the section of the site that has been created in WML. It is also possible to translate HTML pages through the WAP server, although it is likely that not all pages will display properly. People will need to design websites for the new technology.

A WAP phone

As mobile phone handset screens change over to pixel-level displays similar to those that are used on computer screens, many of the translation problems disappear.

Mobile phone technology will make use of **SMART** cards to allow electronic banking (see page 93–6). Unlike traditional cards with a magnetic strip that have to be swiped through point-of-sale terminals and rely upon calculations made on a central computer, SMART cards carry out the calculations themselves. This makes the cards cheaper to operate, reduces transaction times and costs, and significantly reduces opportunities for fraud.

The main problem with e-cash is persuading retailers to buy the necessary machines. While e-cash machines themselves are actually cheaper than the machines needed for magnetic cards and require less maintenance, there is no agreed operating standard. As fraud increases, particularly with the ease of cloning plastic cards with traditional magnetic strips, SMART cards are likely to become more popular for security reasons.

Television banking

With the introduction of **digital television**, television banking is likely to grow dramatically. It is forecast that, since 99 per cent of households have televisions, it will be those households who do not have personal computers and modems that will be attracted by home banking and shopping via the television. Soon, there will be hundreds of digital television channels, some of which will be devoted to banking and shopping services. The TV company Sky already uses its interactive **teletext** service via the television.

With Internet searching available through the television, new microprocessor-controlled digital television, and the further integration of communication and computer technologies, it is difficult to say when a television stops being a television and becomes a computer.

Auction–type retailing

Electronic banking has led to a rise in auction-type retailing. What happens is that a potential purchaser, for example of an airline ticket, places a bid for a flight on a particular route. This bid is circulated to a number of airlines, who decide whether

they want to fly the passenger for the price offered. If one of them does, the deal is struck.

Activity:

Design an auction site for use on the Internet.

Threats to traditional banking

One of the threats to traditional banking is a move by some retailers to cut out banks altogether. They believe that people are not so much interested in money as in the products that money buys. Some retailers have launched their own currencies. These currencies are earned by regular customers or for tasks undertaken, for example filling in customer surveys or trying out new products. This is not new – loyalty card schemes have been offered to retail customers for a number of years. Use of the Internet, driven by major retailers, is becoming a means by which people can opt out of traditional cash-based transactions and barter and exchange goods, cutting out banking altogether.

Changes in working practices

One-third of all existing UK bank branches are forecast to close in the short term. It is likely that most of these closures will occur in poorer communities where there is less money changing hands. Until the 1950s, very few lower paid workers in the UK had their own bank accounts. Any available money was kept in a safe place at home.

A recent survey by ICL found that one-third of the population of the UK, Germany and France would now like to conduct home banking through the television. Even more people in Sweden wanted to do this.

Sainsbury's, Tesco, Marks & Spencer, Prudential, Virgin, General Electric, Ford, AT&T and British Gas have all set up banking services using their customer databases. Sainsbury's quickly attracted 900 000 accounts and the Prudential gained £5 billion in deposits within six months of launching Egg. High interest rates funded by the savings secured by using electronic banking attracted customers, but the high take-up led to a loss of £200 million over the first three years.

Setting up in business – modelling and simulation software

When companies apply for a loan from a bank, they often simulate business activity using a computer to forecast whether they are likely to make a profit. The first stage of applying for a business bank loan is the development of a detailed business plan. In order to predict future business activity, companies will use business modelling software. The **business modelling** software could be specialist modelling software, or it could be a spreadsheet.

Companies are not alone in using modelling software in this way. The Chancellor of the Exchequer uses modelling software to forecast movements in the UK economy and make decisions about how much the

government can afford to spend on things such as education and the National Health Service.

Modelling software enables the user to ask questions such as 'What would happen if I did this …?'. In effect, the modelling software is used to create a 'virtual' company on the computer and allows the user to explore the effect of different decisions on the virtual company before having to suffer the consequences of such decisions on a real business.

A set of **equations** that will best describe the likely behaviour of the business are entered into the modelling software. Without these equations, it would not be possible to carry out a **business simulation**.

Activity:

Design a system based upon spreadsheet software to develop a business plan.

It is possible that the equations will be wrong. Where a business has not yet started, forecasts are based on guesswork. Even a fairly simple model can contain a lot of equations, often referred to as rules. If just one rule is not always true, results of the model will be inaccurate.

A company may not have taken into account all of the factors when constructing its model. For example, an important company member might be unable to work for a month. Most models can be seriously affected by random events such as illness, equipment failure or bad weather.

The data used in constructing a model is vitally important. If you input the wrong data, the answers that come out will be wrong. Even if the data is accurate, a model or simulation cannot guarantee what will actually happen. Only the real event will achieve this.

Electronic payment systems

Nowadays, goods may be paid for using a variety of methods – cash, cheque, credit card where the credit card company pays the bill on your behalf and you then repay the credit card company at a later date, and debit cards where the money is taken directly from your bank account. Cheques, credit cards and debit cards all make use of electronic systems.

Magnetic ink character readers and magnetic ink character recognition

Magnetic ink character recognition (MICR) is used in banking. Magnetic ink characters are the numbers found along the bottom of cheques. They show the customer's account number, branch code and cheque number. The characters are printed using an ink that contains iron and may be magnetised. The magnetic pattern of the numbers is read by a magnetic ink character reader.
A standard character set is used to print the numbers, so that comparisons are simple and reading is fast.

MICR is accurate and secure, but it uses expensive equipment and is suitable only for very large-scale applications. This is an advantage in banking as the high cost would make it unlikely that other people would be able to buy the equipment and print their own cheques.

When a person pays a cheque into a bank, the bank must add the amount to the cheque in magnetic ink before the cheque can be passed through the banking system.

Magnetic strips and readers

Most credit and debit cards have a simple magnetic strip which stores a small amount of data, typically the account number and expiry date of the card. The quantity of data that can be stored is limited to 200 bytes of information.

Magnetic strip readers are found at the side of computerised tills and are used to read information contained in the magnetic strips on cards. The readers detect the pattern of magnetisation and convert it to numeric data. Reading is accurate and fast.

The cards work well but are easily damaged. Exposure to a strong magnet, such as those used to remove security tags in shops, can alter the magnetic pattern representing the vital data on a card. The reader will then be unable to pick up the data and the numbers have to be typed in by hand.

A bank debit card

EPOS and EFTPOS terminals

Electronic point of sale (EPOS) terminals are the cash registers commonly found in retail outlets that also act as terminals to the main computer of the retail outlet. Data about goods being sold is fed into the terminals, normally via barcode readers, touch screens and keyboards and, as well as providing customers with itemised bills, these systems also generate useful management information.

Electronic funds transfer at point of sale (EFTPOS) terminals are similar to EPOS terminals but with some additional features. They are able to transfer funds from a customer's bank account direct to a retailer's bank account after reading the customer's debit card. This provides a much faster method of payment than cheques and credit cards.

The benefits of EPOS and EFTPOS include faster transfer of money to retailers' accounts, reduced loss from cheque fraud and less cash held on retail premises. This reduces the chance of a break-in. Today, it is possible to transfer funds from one account to another almost anywhere in the world instantly.

There is a risk, however, of debit cards being stolen or forged and some people believe that, like credit cards, they encourage people to spend more.

SMART cards

SMART cards have been available for some time. They are essentially debit cards capable of holding much more information on the user than conventional credit or debit cards. Each SMART card contains a **micro-controller** or chip, which often contains either 8 or 16 kilobytes of memory and the usual 200-byte magnetic strip. Each time the holder uses the card, the terminal it is inserted into collects data about the buyer and his or her purchases, and adds to it.

The chip on the card could easily contain a photo of the holder, his or her fingerprints and even an image of the person's iris. The latest SMART cards contain two chips with a secure communication between them. This increases their capacity, security and function. Large amounts of data can be stored on each card, and governments are looking into SMART cards as identity cards and driving licences that hold various types of personal information, such as career records. They provide an ideal key to electronic commerce and could contain credit, debit and electronic purse (see page 94–5) functions. Several banks have carried out successful trials.

There are fears that information on SMART cards could be accessed without the knowledge of the cardholder. However, SMART cards are designed to be carried around by the cardholder, and until the card is inserted into a reader, no one can access this information.

smart**CARD**

0033 2033 3326 1988 210

A. Simon
02/02   20985647   03

A bank SMART card

Activity:

Devise a system that incorporates SMART card technology.

While SMART cards are undoubtedly more secure than credit/debit cards relying simply on a magnetic strip, some people are still concerned about what use the data might be put to as someone could take the information off the card when it is being used. For example, would the banks be able to sell this information to retailers, etc?

One of the reasons SMART cards have not proved more popular is that customers are afraid of what might happen if they lose the card.

Some SMART cards used for electronic shopping are like credit cards with built-in computers. They work in a similar way to telephone charge cards. Cash is transferred from the customer's bank account to the card. A reader at the shop or in the customer's own computer can deduct money from the **microchip** on the card. The name given to this is an electronic purse or **e-cash** (see below).

France has used SMART cards for a number of years as part of its **Minitel** electronic communication system. France Telecom issues SMART cards for use via the telephone. French TV companies use the cards for pay-by-view television.

The hotel chain Hilton has introduced a 'smart card' for regular customers. The card stores the customer's preferences, for example non-smoking room, twin beds, etc. The information can be updated whenever the customer wishes at a special kiosk. To book in and out of the hotel the customer inserts the card into a special kiosk that issues a room key and directions to his or her room, by-passing queues at the reception desk. (See also the chapter on Use of ICT to aid travel.)

Electronic purses and digital currency

An **electronic purse** is a SMART card that holds electronic cash, or **e-cash**, sometimes called **digital currency**, a replacement for traditional cash. Electronic cash can be used for very small purchases and users simply top up the SMART card with the amount of money they wish to carry in a similar way to adding notes and coins to a traditional purse or wallet.

E-cash was initially designed for secure payments from any personal computer to any other workstation, over the Internet. It allows customers to withdraw electronic cash from a bank and store it on their local computer.

Electronic purses are in use in a number of parts of the world, and are particularly successful among students who find a card easier to carry than traditional cash. One card can hold details of a number of different accounts and the customer can transfer funds between accounts easily. Alongside traditional shopping, electronic cash is ideal for Internet trading.

 Activity:

Devise a system to calculate automatically the value of cash in different currencies.

Cardholders can spend digital cash with anyone who will accept the currency. The big advantage of this system is that you do not need to open an account with a particular store, and you do not need to commit any credit or debit card details over the Internet.

The ideas used in SMART cards are already widely used. Most people in the UK already have SMART cards as they are used in **GSM** mobile phones and for satellite television.

In telephone technology, it is commonplace to purchase a card containing credits that can be used for telephone calls from a public or mobile telephone.

Some companies make more money from unspent credits left on cards than from their profit margins on actual use of the cards.

Electronic purses are already being used in a number of British schools to pay for bus fares, school meals and tuck shop purchases. School pupils do not have to carry cash, parents do not have to find small change, the school does not have to handle large amounts of cash on the premises, and

fears of money-related bullying or theft are removed.

Cash machines and SMART cards

The installation of cash machines worldwide has led to other interesting developments. In some countries, parts of the population are illiterate. To give them access to the machines, SMART cards are used and personal identity is confirmed by fingerprint and a pulse reader. The name given to this is biometrics (see page 99). Interestingly, a recent survey has found that 76 per cent of all users would prefer a finger or hand scan to remembering **PINs (personal identity numbers)**. Where fixed lines are not available, cash machines have to use radio wave telecommunications.

Using electronic purses in Siberia

Workers in Siberia in Russia were regularly being robbed on the bus home after they had collected their week's wages. Because of the remote location, law enforcement authorities found it impossible to stop the robbers. The remote location also led to another problem: getting sufficient notes and coins to the wages office. The electronic purse was found to be an ideal solution to both these problems. Wages are now transferred electronically to workers' accounts; the workers make withdrawals from their accounts on to their electronic purses; the electronic purses are locked using a personal code number and, if they should be stolen, can be cancelled immediately and new cards issued with the workers' wages untouched.

The telecommunications company Cellnet is developing a system that will enable mobile phone users to top up their electronic purses using their mobile phone system.

Security

One of the biggest problems facing all types of banking and retailing is fraud. Credit and debit cards may be stolen and used illegally to buy goods and services. The lack of security is the main reason that people give for not banking or paying money over the Internet. They fear that their credit/debit card details may be accessed by unauthorised users. Electronic security is now an important part of the work of the banking and finance sector.

Credit and debit card security

Credit and debit card systems usually continuously map the customer's use of the card. The bank records where you use your card and how much use you make of it over time. If buying habits change, the bank often refuses to accept the purchase until it has spoken to the customer. Other security measures include photographs on cards and **personal identity numbers (PINs)** which only the user knows.

Activity:

Explore a range of security measures that can be put in place to prevent fraudulent use of credit/debit cards.

Visa, the world's largest credit card group, says that it is not aware of any confirmed reports of Internet credit card crime, although it admits that it has heard of some unconfirmed reports. This could be due to the fact that criminals tend to go where the money is. Currently, this is not in Internet sales.

Supermarket loyalty cards can be targeted by criminals. In 1996, the *Independent* newspaper published reports of frauds amounting to £5000 per day committed by teenagers making fake credit cards out of store loyalty cards by reprogramming the magnetic strip. Most shops now use **encryption** systems with their cards (see below).

Alongside secure electronic transfer (SET) of money, there are some other ways to combat fraud. Debit-based systems (where customers enter a bank cash machine PIN), electronic cheques and virtual smart cards are the most common.

Encryption

The only way to protect financial or any other confidential data, and make it readable only to authorised persons, is to use **cryptography** and a very long **password**. The name given to this is **encryption**, which means the adding of a **code**.

Activity:

Devise a secure system for transferring confidential information.

Adding code

People have used code in various forms in the past, from Morse code to the secret codes used to send messages during World War II. With computers, messages can be **encrypted** – put into code – with very little effort. In order to encrypt data, you need an encryption key understood by both the sender and the recipient (receiver) of the message. There are usually two types of encryption key, the **public key** and the **private key**.

Most modern encryption methods are based on mathematical calculations. You can send a message to anyone using the recipient's public key. Anyone interested in security is likely to include this public key in their messages, so you can take it from one of their messages. Most public keys are a long string of digits and letters, basically very long numbers.

The encryption process works by converting the letters of a message into a number using specialised software. The software then performs a complex calculation with the numbers of the converted message, and the recipient's public key. The result can then be sent electronically.

The message can be decoded only by using a private key which corresponds to the recipient's public key. By using this method, any sender can use a public key to encrypt a message, but only the owner of the corresponding private key can decrypt it.

Alternatively, someone can give out their public key and encrypt their own outgoing message with their private key, enabling anyone receiving the message to check that it is really from the named sender. The sender's public key would be used to check the message.

Of course, the larger the numbers used, the more secure the transaction.

This type of encryption is being used for a wide range of applications, including electronic payments and share dealing. It is used wherever companies or individuals want to keep electronic messages private and secure. But is this enough?

Most cryptographic programs just transform data into an unreadable encrypted form, saving it as a 'normal' file. If someone takes a look at that file, they will soon understand that it is an encoded message – since it doesn't have any meaning – and will try to break the code.

Hiding files

To overcome this, some of the latest encryption programs encrypt and hide files in other files called carriers which look like ordinary messages. First, they encrypt the sensitive data using a password and **cryptosystem (algorithm)**. After the encryption, the text will be inserted in the carrier. The resulting carrier (which contains the real message) can be attached to an e-mail message (which is a fake message), or published on a web page near hundreds of other pictures (or other carriers) from where the addressee (the only person who knows which is the right image) can download it without revealing his or her identity.

This method has the advantage of making the message almost invisible, and considerably increases the work of any experienced code-breaker, who must first find the right carrier, remove the message from it, and only after that (if he or she gets this far) begin the hard work of breaking the code.

The most commonly used encryption system is data encryption standard (DES), but this has been used since 1975 and is rather outdated. Although the DES system has been strengthened, and a new version known as triple DES introduced, it does not entirely prevent hacker entry.

The credit card company Visa uses a 128-key encryption code. The most widely used of the newer encryption systems is secure electronic transaction (SET). This also uses 128-key encryption and was developed by Visa, Mastercard, IBM and Commerzbank. The main problem with this encryption system is that while it protects financial data, it does not protect other types of confidential information. Secure socket layer (SSL) is an alternative secure system and, in Germany, Dresdner Bank has developed HBCI, which has now been adopted by almost all German businesses.

Another method of encryption is named after its inventors, Rivest, Alderman and Shamir – the RAS system. One of the latest systems is based on an elliptical curve. It was developed as a specific encryption for mobile telephones. At present, companies are investing heavily in yet another system, known as PKI (public key infrastructure). In the UK, Consignia (the Post Office), supported by the Department for Education and Employment, has taken a lead in developing PKI. The government wants to use the system for tax returns and job seekers.

With so many systems of encryption, and no overall standard to control them, the whole question of data security needs sorting out and standardising.

The real problem is no longer a lack of security as total security is possible, but too much security. Governments want encryption systems that they can intercept. This is due to their concern that organised crime is using the Internet.

The law and encryption

In certain countries, such as the United States, government policy is not in favour of encryption as it believes that the ability to send secret messages would encourage crime. Spain bans it completely. France forbids it without written permission and the Americans have tried to ban the export of the most secure systems. In reality, the nature of the Internet cannot prevent a customer in Madrid buying goods in Britain and therefore using encryption services.

There are of course people who want to watch your every move, often in the name of law and order. This form of observation is called surveillance.

Surveillance and privacy

Security guards monitor closed circuit TV screens

There are a number of different forms of surveillance, from the closed circuit television (CCTV) cameras that cover our towns and cities to loyalty cards and databases that build up details about our lives. ICT-based surveillance has become a central part of our lives. Without it, we would not be able to open a bank account, get an overdraft, or a mortgage. Most surveillance is based on collecting information about an individual or situation that may be analysed later.

The best known surveillance method is CCTV. CCTV is often used to help prevent crime and to monitor traffic flow. As the number of CCTVs grows, civil liberty groups are becoming more concerned about private individuals being watched by governments, and by non-government organisations such as private companies.

Alongside CCTV cameras are a host of other surveillance systems such as speed cameras and traffic monitoring **sensors**. There are even reports of global telecommunications surveillance which monitors all telephone calls and text transfers.

People are happy to have more security brought about by CCTV and an increase in surveillance, but they do not like the idea of always being watched. Most people choose to ignore the growing number of CCTV cameras and other surveillance techniques that are being introduced every day. There are, however, some people who consider these increases in surveillance to be an invasion of their privacy.

The groups of people who monitor privacy issues are known as civil rights groups.

When you visit your local bank, you are likely to be 'watched' by cameras and also through the transactions you carry out on your accounts.

We cannot talk about surveillance without thinking about privacy. Britain has signed up to two international agreements that are relevant here: the **Universal Declaration of Human Rights** and the **European Convention for the Protection of Human Rights**. The European Convention gives us the right to challenge alleged breaches of the privacy law.

Biometrics

It is not just CCTVs that are causing concern to civil rights campaigners. **Biometrics** is a method used to capture measurements of the human body that are unique to an individual. The police have used fingerprints for years to identify criminals. Modern biometric databases can contain iris (eye) prints and DNA information that can identify individuals without doubt.

It is likely that banks will be able to use some of this technology to improve **security** when people make financial transactions. The problem is that, when the information is being used for a good reason, people are not concerned. But would you want such personal information about you to be held ready for any kind of use or to be sold to someone else without your knowledge?

Using the Internet to obtain financial information

The Internet has widened our access to a variety of financial services. It has allowed us to obtain vast amounts of financial information easily and at little or no cost. Anybody with a computer and an Internet connection is able to gain access to information previously available only to large companies and professionals.

For example, we can use the Internet to:

- research companies
- obtain free company annual reports
- compare financial service providers and products
- buy and sell shares
- discuss finance and investment with others in newsgroups, mailing lists and bulletin boards
- purchase investment books and software
- get real-time share prices and information on share volumes and trades.

Activity:

Design a website to help users collect financial data from companies via the Internet.

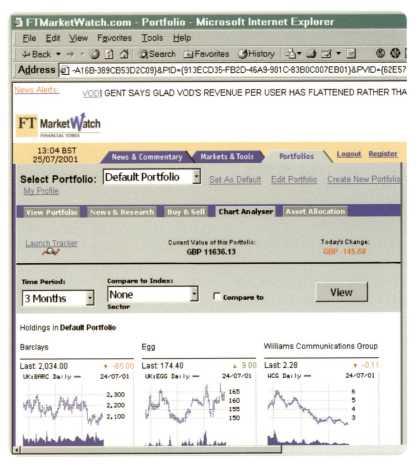

A web-based shares bulletin board

Investment portal sites and bulletin boards

A portal is a website designed for people to visit when they are looking for links to other sites. There are several **portal sites** providing UK investors with financial and investment information. Many of them supply basic information services free, and more in-depth features for a monthly fee. A number of **bulletin boards** exist to enable investors to discuss shares and investment with each other.

Activity:

Design a bulletin board that can be used in the banking sector.

The busiest free bulletin board for UK shares is the Hemmington Scott Information Exchange.

Sites like Electronic Share Information (ESI), Interactive Investor and FT Quicken provide share trading information, bulletin boards, share prices, company news information and forecasts, and portfolio tracking. (A portfolio is a holding of bonds or shares, usually in more than one company. Owners of share portfolios usually like to watch stock market movements in the value of their holdings.)

MoneyeXtra and Moneyworld also offer portfolio tracking, share prices and other stock market information, and are very useful for doing price comparisons to search for best buys in personal loans, credit cards, mortgages and savings accounts.

Motley Fool UK is an excellent site on UK shares and investing, particularly for beginners. It offers company analysis and suggested portfolios as well as market news and comment. Other features include numerous bulletin boards, a portfolio tracker and a useful glossary of financial terms.

Activity:

Design a shares service Internet site suitable for teenagers.

Selling personal information

In the banking industry, several companies specialise in reselling personal information for credit reference purposes. Companies use these records to decide whether an individual may borrow money or take out a credit card.

There are already a number of companies selling surveillance information about how an individual has used the Internet. They gain the information using devices called **cookies**. There are already over 100 million cookies scattered around the world. The information gathered includes who you are, what you have bought, which sites you have visited, how long you stayed there and how often you revisit sites.

Cookies

A cookie is a small piece of information sent by a web server to store on a web browser so it can later be read back from that browser.

Cookies are generated by a web server and stored in the user's computer, ready for future access. They are embedded in the HTML information flowing back and forth between the user's computer and the servers. Web browsers often send out information to sites viewed without the user's knowledge.

Some cookies are useful for having the browser remember specific information such as passwords and user IDs. You could for example develop an online ordering system using cookies that would remember what a person wants to buy. If a person spends one hour ordering CDs at your site, that person could log off and return weeks or even years later and still have those items in the shopping basket.

When you browse the Internet and visit a range of pages that interest you, each of your visits to a page is recorded as a **hit**.

Site tracking by means of cookies can show website owners the places in their website that people go to and then wander off because they don't have any more interesting links to hit. It can also give more accurate counts of how many people have been to pages on their site – in other words, how many hits a page has had.

However, because cookies monitor your Internet use, a lot of people think they are an invasion of privacy. The main concern is that all this is done without anyone's knowledge. Some people may find the gathering of any information unacceptable as they do not know who is collecting what information, and for what purpose.

Some people do not believe that anyone should have the right to collect information about them without their knowledge.

Cookies are also used by companies for targeted marketing. This is probably one of the main uses of cookies. The cookies can be used to build up a profile of where you go and what adverts you click on. This information is then used to target adverts at you, which marketing companies think are of interest. Companies also use cookies to store which adverts have been displayed so the same advert is not displayed twice.

How cookies work

A **command line** in the HTML of a document tells the browser to set a cookie of a certain name or value. Here is an example of some script used to set a cookie:

Set-Cookie: NAME=VALUE; expires=DATE; path=PATH; domain=DOMAIN_NAME; secure

Cookies are usually run from **CGI scripts**, but they can also be set or read by **Javascript**.

Cookies are based on a two-stage process:

1. The cookie is stored in your computer without your knowledge or consent. The web server creates a specific cookie when you access a site. The cookie is essentially a tagged string of text containing your preferences, and the server transmits this cookie to your computer. Your web browser receives the cookie and stores it in a special file called a cookie list. This happens without any notification or request for permission. As a result, personal information is formatted by the web server,

transmitted and saved by your computer. You can access your cookie list from within the Windows directory.

② The cookie is automatically transferred from your machine to a web server next time you log on to the Internet. Whenever you direct your web browser to display a certain web page from the server, the browser will, without your knowledge, transmit the cookie containing personal information to the web server and from there to the company that set it.

● Requirements for connection to the Internet

A user can have either a permanent Internet connection, or a temporary one. Some business organisations have permanent connections, but it is more common at home to have a temporary connection. It is common to use a modem to provide the link from a personal computer to a service called an Internet Service Provider (ISP), which offers a permanent link, or node, into the Internet. The user's modem will dial the ISP, which maintains what is called a point of presence (PoP) – rather like a reception area. The ISP will check that the user's password is valid before allowing access to its file server, and it will normally offer a range of 'customer services' as well as access to the Internet.

It is usually wise for a user to choose an **ISP** located nearby. In addition to paying some sort of **subscription** to the ISP, the user will often have to pay the cost of telephone charges once his or her modem has provided a connection. (Once the connection is made, the user is said to be **online**.) Local rate telephone calls are cheaper than long distance calls.

The cost of accessing the Internet is being reduced as ISPs and telecommunications companies offer a range of special deals to the millions of people who wish to use the Internet. When setting up an Internet connection, it is always worth shopping around to see who is offering the best deals. Some providers offer free connection and an allocation of free calls. Others offer unlimited calls for a set annual or monthly fee.

The modem is said to be **dialling-up** when it connects to the Internet. In the same way, files sent to the Internet are **up-loaded**, while files taken from the Internet are **down-loaded**. Because of costs involved, the data transmission speed of a modem is particularly important when accessing the Internet. The process of connecting to the Internet is called **logging on**, while terminating the connection is called **logging off**.

Use of ICT to aid travel

Getting from place to place can be difficult in today's busy, time-conscious society.

Activity:

Design an automatic rail signal.

● Airlines and trains

Buying a ticket

Purchasing a rail ticket used to be simple. You simply turned up at the railway station and bought a ticket to your destination. Tickets were usually handwritten. A large number of manual operators worked in stations and managed the rail network.

Even railway signals were manually operated via a system of mechanical levers. The introduction of many different train operating companies and a wide range of special offers to entice people to book rail tickets early has changed all this.

Airlines worked in a similar way, but tickets were usually purchased from travel agents who would make a booking with the airline over the telephone. American Airlines was the first company to offer direct bookings. Its computer systems allowed travel agents to book 24 hours a day, via terminals located in the travel agency. Although they allowed other airlines to display their flight departures free, American Airline flights were always first on the list.

The advantage to American Airlines was considerable. The company was also able to change its prices according to demand while other airlines had to follow.

To ensure fairness, a new system was developed to prevent any airline from gaining unfair advantage over competitors. Airlines paid according to the level of service they required. As soon as the new system, CRS (computer reservation system), was introduced, hotel chains, car rental companies and train operators started to use it also, and it was renamed GDS (global distribution system).

Very rapidly, thousands of travel agencies in the USA joined the system and new systems such as SABRE and APOLLO (both GDS systems) started to sell their services across Europe. European airlines, suspicious of what they saw as a take-over from the USA, joined together and developed their own GDS systems.

By making booking prices cheaper to travel agents who used the new GDS systems, within a short period of time, up to two million rail and air fares were being booked in this way.

To the airline or train operator, the system was a great success. The travel agent would type all of the customer details direct into the airline's or train operator's database, saving time and effort.

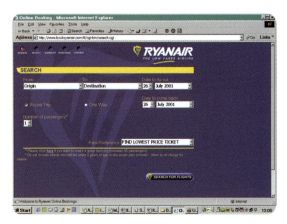

An online booking system

Internet booking systems

Today, direct connection via the Internet allows customers to book flights and rail tickets without the need for a travel agent. This means too that no agency fees are paid. Improved communications and **bandwidths** have enabled the transfer, not only of booking data, but also of full colour pictures, graphics and sound. Airlines are already working on the addition of video clips of destinations. A system where the customer will be able to see inside the aircraft and select a seat, and have a **virtual visit** to hotels, is being developed.

The Internet has enabled UK train operators to sell tickets for a journey from London to Edinburgh to someone in an office in Athens. Major airlines often sell empty seats at heavily discounted rates over the Internet one or two days prior to departure. Some airlines even sell tickets by auction-bidding from potential customers (see page 90).

(see page 90)

Activity:

Explore a rail or flight timetable and a system that can help draw up a workable schedule.

With advances in ICT, travel agents may soon be a thing of the past. Booking travel online is becoming easier every day as train, airline and hotel operators move to this new way of selling.

There is a wide range of travel information available on the Internet, as follows:

- Air travel – most airlines offer online booking facilities. There are also booking agents who deal with all of the airlines through 'flight shops'.

- Rail travel – most travel operators allow you to find times and reserve seats for train journeys online. There are also travel shops offering online booking for all train companies.

- Hotels – a large number of hotels have their own websites. There are also many web-based hotel booking agents. Most hotel chains have their own online booking services.

- Guides – there are a several well-known travel guides on the Internet. Tourist information offices also have websites.

- Booking at short notice – a large number of sites are aimed at offering low-priced, last-minute holidays. Some of these sites even offer online auction systems for last-minute flights and holidays.

Promoting a website

Once an Internet site has been designed, it needs promoting so that people know about it. Booking systems like SABRE may be well known to the airlines themselves, but they mean nothing to the average consumer. One way to become known is to advertise heavily. Advertisements can take many forms: television, newspapers or on other Internet sites. Some travel companies even place advertisements on the most visited Internet pages, for example **search engine** pages.

Activity:

Explore ways of promoting an Internet site.

An alternative is to ensure that the website is registered with the major search engines. Registration with search engines has grown into a business itself. Companies that promote sites on the Internet are known as cyber agents.

Activity:

Explore ways of promoting an Internet site through search engines.

Checking you are who you say you are

One of the biggest difficulties with online booking is knowing the identity of the purchaser. It is easy to do this when someone visits a travel agent because even if the person lies about who he or she is, closed-circuit television cameras can record exactly what an individual looks like.

Activity:

Design a way of checking the identity of someone over the Internet.

False bookings can cost airlines and train operators dearly. Airline and train companies are concerned about the security implications of opening their central reservations (bookings) systems to the public. There are already incidents of bookings being altered, data deleted and information being stolen. Some of this could have happened accidentally, but it could also be done deliberately by rival organisations or by computer hackers.

Firewalls

To prevent data corruption, reservation systems are protected by firewalls. These prevent unauthorised access and restrict the flow of information.

Activity:

Explore ways of protecting a site using a firewall.

Getting busy – Internet traffic jams

Another difficulty faced by the airlines and train operators is the amount of traffic that is generated by opening up their systems to home users. Controlling **data flow** and bandwidth to enable instant access to a few hundred travel agents is easy compared with simultaneous access by a hundred thousand users per day. Companies needed to invest huge amounts of money in upgrading their reservation systems to cope with this demand.

Most of the forty million plus people who access their sites are browsers, not people booking travel. Students and teachers hungry for information form a large number of these browsers. Business travellers who represent a major part of the revenue of these companies do not want to waste time searching for flights on the Internet if a travel agent can do the job faster. Unfortunately for the airlines and train operators, the browsers have more time to spend blocking up the system.

Why book on the Internet?

Activity:

Design an Internet-based booking system.

One of the greatest advantages to someone booking a flight or rail ticket on the Internet is the ability to compare operators, both in terms of price and service.

As more and more people book via the Internet, other changes occur. When a customer books through a travel agent, he or she may pick up a brochure advertising a range of holiday options. In booking via the Internet, this opportunity is lost. However, travel websites are developing opportunities for virtual visits to travel destinations that can show viewers a lot more than a brochure can.

Teletext travel pages

Teletext, the television-based information system, has also proved invaluable to airlines and train operators. It is estimated that in the UK alone, 17.4 million people tune into Teletext every week, with 5.6 million searching the travel pages. People are attracted by the Teletext service partly because it is free, unlike the Internet. Also, more people have televisions.

Travel companies use Teletext to offer last-minute bargains to fill up spaces they have left. Information can be updated instantaneously, allowing companies to offer departures even within 24 hours. On average, over 1000 updates are made to the travel pages every day. Another advantage to operators is that they can use this form of advertising anonymously. All that is shown is the destination, date of departure, place of departure, duration and price. This is very important to some operators who do not want to be seen as discounting their products.

Use of ICT to aid travel

Last-minute holiday bargains advertised on Teletext

Activity:

Design a Teletext system that could be used by a rail or airline operator.

Other digital media

Some travel companies are using CD-ROMs to sell travel. A CD-ROM can be used to store all kinds of data, including rail timetables, flight details, sounds and pictures.

Each travel operator can create its own television-style holiday programme on CD-ROM. Although CD-ROMs cannot easily be updated, they offer the operator a low-cost way of promoting their own products and information that they want the viewer to see. CD-ROMs are a cheaper option than printing holiday brochures, and they allow the viewer to hear the crashing waves on the local beach, as well as seeing the picture. It is estimated that the production of a CD-ROM costs approximately one-third that of a paper brochure.

Activity:

Design and produce a CD-ROM promoting your local area.

Local tourist offices are helping to produce some CD-ROMs. Some tour operators are producing CD-ROMs in the form of an educational game.

Activity:

Use ICT to design and produce a folded leaflet advertising your local area.

Ticketless travel

Another major change brought about by new technology is the revolution in ticket production. Airlines and train operators have known for years that they have spent large amounts of money issuing paper tickets that are often swapped for boarding passes at check-in. Traditional carbon copy tickets are very expensive to produce. Carbon copy multi-part tickets are also time-consuming at check-in.

Activity:

Design a ticket-issuing system that can produce traditional multi-part carbon copy tickets.

Air travel

The airlines introduced ticketless travel in the 1990s and quickly discovered a saving of nearly 30 per cent of their distribution costs.

Low-cost airlines (such as easyJet and Ryanair) use this system to offer low-price fares. The biggest difficulty faced by airlines in offering ticketless services is that they are legally obliged under the terms of the Warsaw Convention to notify passengers of certain information, for example the airline's liability in the event of an accident. To overcome this problem, airlines will often use a fax machine, printout or **downloadable** booking form to carry this information. This is still cheaper to them than issuing a ticket.

The International Air Transport Association (IATA) has developed a standard for electronic tickets. The intention is to allow passengers with an electronic ticket to travel on any airline for which their fare is valid. SMART cards are also being developed and British Airways has issued an executive club card that can be used in an automatic machine. A further advantage of ticketless travel is that it removes the problems associated with refunds. For example, it is no longer necessary to retrieve unused tickets from customers.

While it would be possible to have a SMART travel card with a built-in processor for use with any travel company, it is unlikely that the airlines will want to lose their corporate identity in this way.

Rail travel

Train operators often use credit card-sized tickets for domestic rail travel as these are the only tickets that will operate automatic barriers. It is likely, however, that these will be replaced eventually by SMART cards that can be reused. SMART cards would allow train operators to track passenger movements for the first time.

One of the difficulties facing the introduction of SMART cards is that of getting the various train operators to agree on a standard format.

Activity:

Design a ticket-issuing system that can make use of magnetic strips on tickets.

SMART cards have been piloted by London Transport, where five bus companies, more than 75 travel card-issuing outlets and 19 underground stations agreed to offer a card recharging service. It is intended that the cards be sold through sweet shops, tobacconists and newsagents. (For more information on SMART cards, see pages 93–4.)

Catching fare dodgers

London Underground is also using new technology to reduce the £30 million it loses through fare dodgers each year. Eighteen thousand on-the-spot £10 fines per week can be issued. The computerised system can be used to read the penalty notices, process payments, issue reminders and track fines. As most of these penalty notices are handwritten, an **optical character recognition scanner** is needed to read the notices.

Activity:

Design a system that could track people issued with on-the-spot fines and issue reminder notices.

Use of ICT to aid travel

Activity:

Explore a system that could interpret handwritten addresses and names.

Using the road

New technologies are also widely in use in road transport. Areas range from traffic control in our cities and the development of an Intelligent Vehicle Highway System (IVHS) to the rescue services.

Roadside **sensors** are used to pick up signals from passing cars to allow control of speed and road use. Some cars are already being fitted with **satellite navigation** and devices that automatically pick up traffic warnings.

Pay-as-you-drive schemes

For some years, governments have been exploring **pay-as-you-drive** schemes to cut down on road congestion. The technology already exists for cars to be fitted with sensors that track mileage and journey details. It would be possible to introduce a pay-as-you-drive system with various charges according to the time of day. It could be cheaper, for example, to drive from A to B before 8 am or after 9.30 am. Such schemes are seen as a method of not only relieving traffic congestion, but of persuading people to travel less and reduce the harmful effects of emission gases in the atmosphere.

The mileage could be paid for using a SMART card or, as in Singapore, via a pre-paid card that is inserted in a slot on the dashboard. The pre-paid card can be pre-loaded with cash at a petrol station or shop and cash is automatically deducted as

the driver passes under sensors placed along the road. Failure to insert a card results in an automatic penalty, which is enforced when a photograph is taken of the car's registration plate.

Road rescue services

Emergency rescue services carrying out roadside repairs

All of the road rescue services are now dependent upon ICT. A user pays an annual subscription or fee to belong to the rescue service. The subscription is usually based on a number of options for the level of rescue cover, for example home start, roadside assistance, vehicle recovery, European cover and personal cover.

Let's look at one rescue:

- A UK driver with a family of four has a car breakdown in southern France. The driver has full membership of the rescue service, including European cover.

- The driver telephones the rescue service, which sends out the nearest local recovery agent with a rescue vehicle.

- The mechanic assesses whether the vehicle can be fixed on the spot and if not, the car and passengers are taken to the recovery agent's base.

- The recovery agent assesses the vehicle and notifies the rescue service in the UK.

- The car is booked into the nearest franchise dealer for repair.

- A taxi is provided to take the family to the nearest car hire agent, where a hire car is booked on their behalf.

- As their own car cannot be fixed in time for their return home, the family has to drive to Calais, where they swap the French hire car for an English hire car.

- They travel home and return the hire car at a local UK base.

- Five days later, the driver returns to France by plane to collect the repaired car.

To make an effective rescue possible, the company needs a range of comprehensive **databases**. These include customer details and access to a wide range of other resources such as car hire companies, airlines, repair garages and recovery agents. The company also needs to track carefully the progress of any customer's case. There is, of course, an added problem in that the customer is likely to be upset, and any delay or inaccuracies are likely to make the situation worse.

New technology will also be needed to locate the customer, both in terms of mobile telephones and mapping.

Activity:

Design a system or part of a system that could be used by a rescue service.

Supporting the driver

Formula One cars partially controlled through radio communications with engine maintenance systems located in pit-stop areas

New technology has enabled some car manufacturers to go a step further in terms of supporting the driver. Having first developed anti-theft devices which give out radio signals locating the car's exact position and informing the local police, the latest devices can even disable a stolen car. **Monitors** and sensors can also be connected direct to a customer assistance centre to enable garages to monitor engine performance. These sensors can be used not only to monitor breakdowns before they occur, but also to enable garages to modify engine performance while a car is being driven. The systems were originally designed for use in Formula One racing cars.

Data from a vehicle's on-board **diagnostic system** enables garages to adjust timing and improve mileage to suit a specific petrol. The car manufacturer Porsche is working with the computer company Siemens to develop this system further.

General Motors has even developed a system where, when the airbag in a vehicle is activated, the rescue company phones the driver on his or her mobile phone to check if all passengers are safe. If driver and phone cannot answer for any reason, the rescue services are automatically sent to the exact location of the vehicle.

Other sensors include on-board **cameras** and **radar** which can detect when a car is heading for a solid object. If the driver does not apply the brakes, the car applies the brakes independently. Sensors have been developed to warn drivers of low tyre pressure and even to poke the driver in the back if the car senses that the driver is falling asleep. As the technology develops, it is likely that drivers will not need regular miles-based service schedules. Remote garages will determine the need for a service according to engine performance and will be able to make some of the changes remotely.

Use of ICT in urban traffic control

A traffic junction is controlled by ICT

Our roads and motorways are becoming busier and busier and, without information systems to control junctions and pedestrian crossings, accidents would be much more frequent, especially in congested town centres. Most large towns have an **urban traffic control system** that operates traffic lights at road junctions and pedestrian crossings, and controls the flow of traffic through the town. These systems can normally work in one of a number of different **modes**, according to the time of day and how busy the road system is. Traffic flow is carefully monitored and logged using sensors and the traffic control centre can use a range of techniques to keep the traffic moving, such as controlling lights and pedestrian crossings.

Data logging and control software

Control is about making things work as you want them to. Software can control movement. For example, it can control the movement of a robot connected to it, the opening of doors in a high security area, control points on the rail network or the movement of a screen image. Feedback – data logged by sensors – is often used to inform a **control system**.

Data is often collected automatically by **sensors** and **remote sensors**, and processed at a later date. In some cases, data collected by a sensor is used to bring about an immediate outcome *and* is also used at a later date for a different purpose. An example is the sensors that are placed just under the road surface at junctions to record the volume of traffic.

The data collected has an immediate effect on traffic lights at the junction, and is used later in traffic control offices to monitor road use. **Data logging** describes the automatic recording of traffic data as it is produced.

There are two main types of data loggers:

- Data loggers with **permanent computer connections**. These take readings and then send them to the computer via a wire or electronic signal. The computer can process the readings at once to produce an outcome, or store them on disk for processing at a later date.

- Data loggers with **temporary computer connections**. These are less expensive than those with permanent computer connections and are ideal for monitoring data such as environmental conditions at weather stations over a period of time. As with all data loggers, the sampling interval, or time between readings, can be varied. The time over which logging takes place can be changed too.

The hardware, and associated software, that links data logging sensors with a computer is called an **interface**, or **buffer box**.

An interface compensates for the difference in operating characteristics (speeds, codes, etc.) between the sensors and computer. Sensors can be linked to the interface box, which is then linked to the computer. The software is loaded, and the computer will know which sensors it is connected to. The buffer facility can hold data temporarily to allow for any difference in speed between sensor and computer.

Where the device that is being controlled by a control system is located outside the computer, for example traffic lights at a junction, an interface is used in the same way to link the computer to the lights that produce the outcome (red/amber/green) of data logging.

Control devices

Output can be used to control devices such as lights, buzzers, robots and actuators (hardware devices such as motors). The output operates parts such as switches and hydraulic systems in these devices. For example, an actuator motor might be used to open a window in a greenhouse when a temperature sensor has registered that it has got too hot.

Road traffic control room linked via buffer boxes to traffic sensors

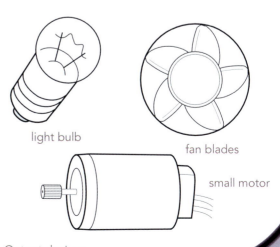

light bulb

fan blades

small motor

Output devices

The capture and storage of data for a data logging system is called data acquisition. The data is collected through sensors. Sensors are input devices that are used to detect external changes in an environment. They may for example register levels of light, temperature, sound, proximity, position, pH balance in the soil, or humidity.

Sensors are often located at some distance from the computer system to which they are sending data. In this case they are known as remote sensors. Their electronic signals are sent through telephone wires or via radio transmitters to a computer that could be located in another part of the world.

Remote sensors are used in traffic control systems and weather stations, where temperature, pressure, traffic flow and wind speed can be detected at many isolated locations, and the data then sent to a central computer. In a similar way, water authorities may use remote sensors to monitor the level of water or pollution in rivers and reservoirs.

Types of sensor

- **Light sensors** have a number of uses. They are used in road systems to detect low light. This enables street lights to be turned on automatically and also enables traffic lights to be brighter during daylight hours than at night. Light sensors can also be used to sense car headlights.

- **Sound sensors** can be used to record the level of sound. They can be used to control sound levels in places like nightclubs.

- **Temperature sensors** are one of the most common types of sensor as they are used in central heating systems, refrigerators, etc.

- **Proximity sensors** are usually in two halves. If the halves are moved away from each other, they activate a signal. They are ideal for burglar alarms.

- **Humidity sensors** sense the amount of moisture present in the air or soil.

- **Pressure sensors** detect any change in pressure. They can be built into door mats as part of an intruder alarm system or to open automatic doors. They can also be built into road surfaces.

- Most **movement sensors** are microwave sensors. Where traffic lights are set to be controlled by the flow of traffic, microwave sensors are used where it is not possible to lay cables in the road. They are commonly known as radar sensors.

- **Infra-red sensors** detect a presence, such as a person waiting at a pedestrian crossing. They are commonly used in alarm systems and security lighting.

- **Magnetic field sensors**. Road traffic systems consist of wires called **loops** that are placed under the road and produce a magnetic field. There are three loops before each traffic light-controlled junction. The loops are 40 volts. The electro-magnetic **impedance** changes as vehicles pass over. This change is measured and enables the traffic control centre to monitor and control traffic flow.

Further common examples of the use of sensors are at traffic lights and pedestrian crossings, to detect the presence of vehicles or people, and in freezer and chiller cabinets in supermarkets, to monitor temperature.

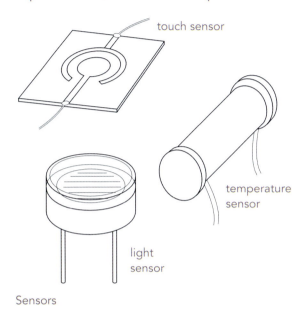

touch sensor

temperature sensor

light sensor

Sensors

Digital and analogue signals

The data received is converted to **digital values** and transmitted to the computer system. The data can be processed immediately, to influence outputs from the system, or it can be stored for later analysis.

Digital values are more accurate than analogue. An electronic device is digital if data in it is represented as electrical 'on' and 'off' signals that correspond to binary digits and can be stored in computer memory. The data is therefore represented as a series of 1s and 0s.

A device is **analogue** where data is represented as signals that vary within a predefined range. Traditional watch faces are analogue. The hands move continuously round a dial, within the predefined range of set seconds (0 to 60), minutes (0 to 60) and hours (12 or 24 in total). Time is represented by the position of the hands on the dial.

Many modern watches have a digital display, in which time is represented by the digits shown on a small display screen.

Digital signals have two advantages:

- They can be copied exactly, without any loss of quality.
- They can be further processed by computer.

All modern, general purpose computers are digital, but analogue computer circuits are used in industrial control equipment.

A digital computer is more accurate than an analogue computer because it only needs to sense the difference between clearly **distinguishable states**. For example, a slight fluctuation in electrical voltage would affect the result in an analogue computer but would not affect a digital computer because it could still easily distinguish the 1 state from the 0 state of any circuit element. For the same reason digital music reproduction (as on a CD) is more accurate than analogue reproduction (on a traditional vinyl record or cassette tape).

Data logging systems

A data logging system has the following characteristics:

- It involves a process monitored by instruments or sensors.

- The sensors are connected to an interface board which is in turn connected to the computer.

- The computer controlling the system samples the readings at regular time intervals.

- Readings are recorded, usually by storing them on a backing store.

- Data is collected over a measured length of time, called the period of logging, and it is analysed. Analysis may take place while logging continues, or at the end of the period.

- Results may be displayed continuously: in printed form, as numbers; as a screen display that updates continuously and as a graph that can be printed. The time interval and period of logging will vary according to the type of data being monitored.

For example, on a heart monitor, heartbeat might be recorded over the period of a patient's stay in intensive care, say a week, and recordings might be taken every minute. In a traffic centre, traffic flow may be recorded throughout an entire year, on a minute-by-minute basis.

Logging modes

Three typical logging modes are used in a traffic control centre:

- vehicle-activated

- fixed-time

- program-controlled.

These modes can be set to run automatically, or can be changed manually from the control centre in special circumstances. For example, in the event of a serious road accident, controllers might want to clear certain roads to allow emergency vehicles to get through, and they might also need to divert traffic from the accident site. A computer chip housed in the microprocessor in the control box located close to each junction bears the program with all the necessary information to control that junction. Each program is specially written at the control centre on the basis of data gathered about the nature of traffic flow through the junction. Each microprocessor is connected to the main computer in the control centre.

Vehicle-activated mode

A traffic control centre

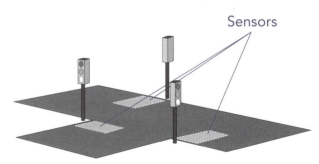

Sensors

vehicle-activated mode sensors in the road detect vehicles approaching traffic lights at junction

Vehicle-activated mode sensors

At quieter times of day, a junction is likely to be in vehicle-activated mode. Sensors sunk into the road surface just before the junction detect when a vehicle is approaching the traffic lights. The data enters the system and, if the lights are already green for that vehicle, they will not change. If the lights are red as the vehicle approaches, they will change to green as long as the system has not detected another vehicle approaching from another part of the junction.

At very quiet times of the day and night, when there are long gaps between passing traffic, most systems will turn the lights to red at intervals of a set number of minutes as a safety precaution.

Fixed-time mode

As traffic flow becomes heavier, the system is likely to change into fixed-time mode because the traffic lights would be changing too often in vehicle-activated mode. The program in the microprocessor will contain a number of different plans to control the timing of the sequence of the lights, according to the time of day. A clock will be built into the microprocessor to enable it to operate the right plan at the right time. Typical plans might be:

- morning rush hour
- morning/afternoon off peak
- evening rush hour
- evening off peak.

The timings used in these plans will have been worked out on the basis of the traffic survey data collected at the junction and throughout the town road system. It is important to remember that the flow of traffic through one junction

will affect the flow through the next junction in the system, and so on. Vehicle movements around the whole town must be carefully coordinated.

Vehicle-activated traffic light system

Program-controlled mode

In a very busy town centre, junctions and pelican crossings are likely to be in program-controlled mode during the busiest parts of the day. All traffic movement will be monitored and controlled by a central computer in the town's control centre.

In a typical town centre, around 45 junctions and 25 pelican crossings may be under the control of the central computer in program-controlled mode.

On each road approaching a junction that is within the system, a detector buried in the road surface will send a signal along a dedicated line to the central computer each time a vehicle crosses it. The computer will know the state of the lights at the junction, and the average speed of a vehicle between the detector and the junction.

It can therefore calculate the flow of traffic for each road in and out of the junction.

The state of the flow of traffic can be displayed on a screen in the control centre, where operators will be able to zoom in on particular road positions if they need to see more clearly what is happening. Unless the operator decides to override the central system, the central computer program will continue to deal with problems of congestion. It will take account of all the data it receives, and will try to create the best flow situation by gradually altering the timing of lights.

The control centre might want to override the system for road works, an ambulance or other emergency situation.

The period of time any light is on a particular colour is often called the **split**, while the time it takes for a set of lights to go through a complete cycle of changes is called the **cycle**. The timings between different junctions are called the **offset**.

Activity:

Design a traffic control or traffic monitoring system.

System faults

It is important that provision is made for system failure, as this could lead to chaos in a busy traffic area. Normally, if the central system fails, traffic lights will automatically revert to fixed-time mode. The fault will be displayed on screen in the control room, and a warning buzzer may sound. Faults will be logged by the computer and can be printed out at any time.

At a quiet time during the night, the computer program will check all parts of the system for faults and the results of these tests will be logged and printed so that engineers can trace any faults and repair them.

Car parking

The traffic control system in a town may also control the information signs about car parks in the central area. **Detectors** placed in the road at the entrances and exits of car parks will send data about vehicle movement to the central computer, which can keep an up-to-date count of the number of vehicles in each car park. It will store information about the total number of vehicles that each car park can take so that the car park signs can display the number of spaces available, or whether the car park is full.

Operators in the control centre will be able to read reports on screen about the status of any one car park, or all the car parks in an area. They will also be able to see whether any detectors are faulty. They will be able to view the message that is currently being displayed on any car park entrance. This will help ensure that all information being given to drivers is accurate.

Modelling and simulation

Transport and travel systems are often modelled or simulated using a **virtual reality** world to build a model where each item has a 'real' position in a three-dimensional (3D) space. Designers try to set up a simulation where each item appears and acts naturally within the **virtual environment**.

It is possible to link virtual reality environments to people by using headsets, gloves and shoes. This enables the user to pick up virtual objects and move around the environment before it is ever built.

The key to any effective traffic control system is to simulate it to check it will work correctly before the system is put into use and causes major traffic problems. Modelling and simulation software is designed to allow the user to ask the question 'What if…?', given a particular set of circumstances. The software allows the creation of a computer model, which can be either a mathematical model or a simulation model.

A computer model contains data and rules. The rules control the way the model works. They are instructions for carrying out calculations, or conditions when particular calculations should be carried out. The model can be of a situation or a process.

Simulation can be used wherever it is too difficult, dangerous or costly to carry out real experiments. Examples include modelling nuclear reactors, experiments in chemistry and training air traffic controllers. Architects use simulations to calculate the stresses involved in buildings and bridges.

It is much cheaper to set up a computer model than to build a whole system for testing. Simulations are also used to crash test cars. It is much cheaper to test a product with a computer simulation than to crash a real car.

Simulation is used to train pilots, astronauts, divers and anyone who will work in situations for which special preparation is required.

Activity:

Explore the systems used in simulations.

The user of a computer model can make changes quickly and easily, to find out what happens if the situation changes. Tests can be repeated as often as the user wishes. If a model or simulation has disastrous results, the user can simply try again.

Simulation models are used in Formula One racing. The performance of a Formula One car is of vital importance and a simulation model will be used to predict how the car's performance might change under certain circumstances, for example if its tyres were changed, or the road had more or fewer bends. In this case, the use of simulation allows situations that could be life threatening to the car driver to be tried out in safety.

Many computer games are simulations. Football game simulations are common and popular, as are flight and driving simulators. Simulation also provides a relatively inexpensive way for games players to experience 'real' exciting situations.

Use of ICT in retailing

Shopping takes place in various ways

In recent years we have been seeing the decline of the small independent specialist shop. Instead, we have an increasing number of large superstores and chains. Today's shops stock thousands of different items from all over the world to meet our needs. A rapidly growing number of people are ordering their goods over the Internet. The growth in use of mobile phones is likely to extend the use of electronic shopping further. But even town centre shops rely more and more on new technology.

Nowadays, all large shops are run **electronically** to make sure that things like re-ordering and stocktaking are done as quickly and efficiently as possible. The shops that do this best are usually the most successful because their IT system enables them to handle a wide range of products.

Having a good range of products in a wide variety of sizes, colours and styles is what attracts customers.

Location and gravity modelling

Shop owners say that the three most important issues for a shop are location, location and location. The shops of the past that proved the most successful were located in places where people walked. Nowadays, being located in a large shopping centre usually ensures that a shop picks up passing customers who are attracted inside by attractive window displays.

Locating a shop in the correct place is very important. Some traders conduct extensive research into the best location for a shop. This research could be based upon prime locations for passing trade, travelling distances for potential customers, car parking, availability of competition in the area and even the first names of people living in the area. In the case of names, research is conducted to see if a link between first names and shopping trends is established. If this link can be established, a system can be developed to explore the best location for a shop. The modelling of systems in this way is called **gravity modelling**. Gravity modelling can be used to explore any link between shopping habits and best location. For example, a shop could be suited more to young, old or busy people or it could be targeted at a particular social economic grouping.

Activity:

Design a database model that could be used to explore the best location of a store to target a specific audience.

To use gravity modelling, potential retailers need to access data. Some of this, for example first names, could be obtained from the electoral register. Other types of information are far more difficult to obtain and can be very controversial. Examples would include the religious beliefs or sexual preferences of shoppers.

Manufacturers as customers (business to business trading)

It is not only consumers who buy goods. Shops have to buy their goods from other suppliers called wholesale suppliers or direct from manufacturers. Manufacturers who supply the shops, wholesalers and other manufacturers themselves have to buy their raw materials and product components, or parts. These range from food ingredients for the catering trade to the electronics components and chips incorporated into almost all of today's products. Unlike the general public, manufacturers do not go to shops to buy their products. They use catalogues, manuals and visits from company representatives to select from different suppliers.

Manufacturers have to keep up to date with new technology, find the best suppliers in terms of quality and price and arrange delivery at the correct time in the manufacturing process. All of these activities have been improved as a result of the introduction of ICT-based systems.

Product catalogues themselves have changed as a result of ICT systems. Updating and printing paper-based catalogues is an expensive and time-consuming process. Catalogues have to be linked to product details and prices. The use of desktop publishing (DTP) systems has improved the presentation of products and has allowed information and prices to be changed fairly easily. The introduction of CD-ROM and online catalogues has helped suppliers to maintain and update catalogues.

Activity:

Design a system for the production of product catalogues. Your catalogue can be paper based, CD-ROM or Internet based.

To help manufacturers to find the best supplier a number of companies have set up specialist services. These companies produce publications on paper, CD-ROM and online, usually specialising in a particular sector, for example the building sector or catering. Their output is similar to publications or directories like *Yellow Pages*.

Activity:

Design an Internet- or database-based system that could be used by a manufacturer to select between different suppliers of similar products.

While some manufacturers search for new suppliers, other manufacturers have built up a good relationship with particular suppliers. For example, a chef working in a restaurant might prefer the quality and taste of an ingredient produced by a single supplier. Suppliers who are used in this way are called preferred suppliers.

Communication between supplier and manufacturer is vital, if we are to have a ready supply of high quality products in the retail outlets we use. Improved communications brought about by the introduction of ICT systems have changed the way products are designed and produced. Some designs for new products are totally modelled and designed in **cyberspace**. ICT enables companies to work together with their preferred suppliers of materials, ingredients and parts to design new products and services. **Concurrent engineering** is the name given to parallel development of products, parts and materials using ICT systems.

Activity:

Explore concurrent engineering and design a communication system that could be used to improve communication between a manufacturer and preferred suppliers.

Manufacturers need to do more than find the best supplier. They need to use ICT to order supplies. Supplies need to arrive in time or production will stop and supplies to the shops we rely upon would dry up. The name given to this is **just in time (JIT)** manufacturing. It reduces manufacturing costs by saving the manufacturer storage and by reducing the time between having to buy the ingredient or component (part)

and being able to recover this outlay by selling the finished product.

Activity:

Explore the ways designers can use the Internet, online product catalogues or CD-ROMs to keep up to date with technological and components development.

Manufacturers have to keep a careful watch over their stocks of components and ingredients to ensure that production does not stop as a result of a shortage of a key item during manufacture. Databases are used to maintain stock levels in manufacturing just as they are in a retail outlet to ensure each product sold is replaced. Sometimes these systems are fully automatic and can order replacements from warehouses and even direct from manufacturers.

Activity:

Design a stock level database for use by a manufacturer or retail outlet.

While suppliers of components and ingredients to manufacturers have never needed a high street outlet, until the introduction of ICT most retailers have. The introduction of better communication systems is now bringing about a change here as well. Today, some retail outlets cannot be found in the high street or shopping centre. They exist only on the Internet. This provides the public with the advantages that have been available to manufacturers for some time. Alternative methods of finding, comparing and ordering products and components are now available to all.

Cyberspace

A shop in cyberspace

The Internet exists in what is called cyberspace. Cyberspace is much cheaper than the land needed to build a real shop in an accessible place. Unlike real shops, where the customers have to go to the location of the shop, in cyberspace, the shop goes to the consumers. The window display is the website.

Some early cyberspace shops were arranged in 'shopping arcades' similar to real shops. It was quickly realised that as location is of little importance in cyberspace, it is better to place similar shops together. When you want a new pair of shoes you want to compare the prices and styles from different retailers selling the same or similar shoes, not struggle your way past other shops selling other products that you do not want. Another name given to Internet shopping is **virtual reality shopping**.

Activity:

Read the section on website design (pages 73–4) and design a shop website of your own.

Activity:

Read the section on managing data (page 2) and the section on designing and constructing databases (pages 5–11) and design a system that would compare prices of similar products sold in a range of shops.

Virtual reality shopping

Virtual reality shopping is being developed by a number of organisations, including the University of Salford, and is being used by some retailers to plan store layouts. It could soon be a way of buying goods from the home and mobile phones. A US company is developing a virtual shop where a customer can not only walk up and down the aisles, picking up and looking at the goods, but can smell, touch and even try on a pair of jeans and see what they look like without leaving home. This is achieved by means of **sensors** fitted in clothing.

Activity:

Research the term virtual reality and show how it could have an impact on shopping in the future.

Unlike shops, where the larger companies can win the space and custom, on the Internet it is the creative, ground-breaking, risk-taking, small organisations who can afford to make less money for a longer time that have been succeeding.

Another big difference is that all of the work on designing shop fronts, window displays, logos and store layout is redundant when looking at selling on the Internet.

Keeping the customers interested

Some shops such as supermarkets use various methods, many of them ICT based, to keep people in the store and encourage them to buy. Tinted windows make it look gloomy outside so less attractive. Special lighting makes people blink less so that they feel sleepy and are more likely to buy. The absence of clocks helps people lose track of time. The smell of freshly baked bread can be pumped into the supermarket to entice people.

You cannot pump the smell of bread over the Internet, as yet, or remove clocks. In **cyberspace**, sellers and shops need to develop new methods such as web pages that attract buyers, are visually interesting and most important of all not too difficult to **navigate**.

Activity:

Design an attractive website for potential customers of fashion items. Your website must be easy to navigate.

To attract buyers, Internet retailers also need to think about the type of computers their customers are likely to have. They have to accept that, unlike a traditional high street which has a limited number of similar shops, on the Internet it is possible to visit hundreds if not thousands of shops.

Electronic shopping could even be considered environmentally friendly as it means fewer trips to the supermarket and shopping centres which could significantly reduce car use. A single delivery van can visit a large number of households.

The opportunity for shoplifting is also reduced on the Internet.

Recent surveys of shoppers suggest that most people think that shopping in a supermarket in particular is both expensive and stressful. The most recent study shows that two-thirds of people dislike the regular visit to the supermarket.

While people will probably always want to visit actual shops to try on clothing, to keep up to date with the latest fashion trends and for one-off large purchases, the purchase of regular items may become largely ICT based.

Buying regular items

Repeat purchases such as breakfast cereals and baked beans could easily be ordered remotely, using existing technology such as the telephone, or even through **remote sensors** inside the fridge, store cupboard and freezer.

Intelligent fridges and freezers have already been developed which automatically order replacement goods when they are used. After all, who needs to touch or smell a tin of beans or box of cornflakes?

Some shops are even joining in the move towards Internet shopping by introducing electronic kiosks. Electronic kiosks sited in stores and other public areas such as railway stations and parks enable shops to reach out and 'capture' more customers who may not live locally.

Activity:

Read the section on control systems (page 112) and design an automatic ordering system for use at home.

Shopping using the self-scan system

Electronic shopping

Supermarket shopping, from the customer's point of view, can be inefficient and inconvenient as it is the customer who does the most work. This involves visiting the supermarket's premises, picking up items from shelves, handling the goods at the shop counter and carrying them home. Sometimes customers even scan their own shopping.

A self-scan system uses a 'boot' which is carried around by the customer who has to be a registered cardholder for that store. Customers insert their card into the boot and whenever they want to buy an item, they scan the barcode with their boot and put the item straight into their bag.

The idea behind the self-scan is to provide more efficient shopping for customers. It saves time queuing at checkouts. Shopping is already bagged up and all the customer has to do is give the boot to the cashier, who downloads the information on to the main computer network which in turn produces a receipt for the customer.

The advantages of this system are that customers can see how much they are spending as they go round the supermarket. If they have a budget, they can keep to it because when they go over it they can just take the item off before they get to the checkout and deduct it from their boot. For security reasons, there are random checks to make sure that no one is taking more items than they have programmed in.

But self-scan systems still require a visit to the supermarket. Digital shopping means that you can shop from home. In the digital age, shops will need to organise the transport and handling. Perhaps, in the future, fancy packaging will become redundant as it will not be necessary to entice people to pick items from among other similar ones on shop shelves.

Changing jobs

Changes in shopping habits could lead to job losses in the packaging industry, but should be more environmentally friendly. The increase in the use of electronic shopping may lead to a reduced number of sales staff, but an increase in the requirement for training of a few hand-picked staff. This is particularly important when considering safety measures for when the technology fails, and in considering the large number of people who still prefer to talk to a human rather than a machine.

Until the 1950s a boy from the butcher's or grocer's would deliver shopping to customers, travelling on a bicycle with a large basket on the front. The self-service supermarket with lower prices and wider ranges of products ended this practice. Now shops are introducing Internet shopping and home deliveries.

To compete, supermarkets will have to introduce more checkouts, bag packers, carry-to-car services and better-trained staff in order to bring back the personal touch. Some supermarkets even provide umbrella patrols on rainy days, and have singles nights. Finally, what supermarkets will really need to address is that many customers want to avoid having to visit them at all.

The impact of new technology means that shops will have to adapt to new channels of competition. There will be an impact on jobs and the environment. There will be a big gap between the technically competent and those who do not keep up with technological development. There will be a psychological effect on those who feel uncomfortable with the technology and an increased remoteness and isolation of individuals sitting behind computers in their homes. The 20 years of decline of high street shops in the UK is likely to become worse as electronic retailing takes sales away from town centres. Some stores will turn from profitable enterprises into loss makers and will have to close.

Activity:

Read the section on input and output devices and design (pages 113–15), and design a system that would be friendlier to someone who is afraid of new technology.

One way that shops can fight back is to make themselves places of social interaction and entertainment rather than centres of consumerism. The Virgin Megastore in Times Square, New York, attracts customers via its café with live performances by pop stars, a four-screen movie theatre and a sports themed restaurant.

Many UK bookshops have areas where customers can sit in comfortable armchairs and drink a cup of coffee while looking at books.

The increase in digital shopping will have a serious impact on jobs, with changes both in the number of people employed, and in the types of jobs they will do. New jobs will be created in areas such as **website design**, **technical maintenance**, **technical support**, database management and e-mail response. These jobs will require totally different skills from those of today's shop assistant.

But for some people, a visit to the supermarket can be the only social interaction in the day. A large number of people like to visit 'real' shops. To be competitive, supermarkets need to keep up to date with new technology so that they know what goods to stock, when to re-order, etc. This is a very complex task requiring the use of EPOS and EFTPOS (see also pages 93 and 128–9).

⬤ ICT in a traditional high street shop

Computer-aided design

Traditional-style high street shops are often designed using **computer-aided design (CAD)** software which simulates or models room or shop interiors. Three-dimensional (3D) models are used regularly by interior designers to show their clients exactly what the product will look like before it is built.

CAD software is designed to make it easier to produce detailed designs and accurate drawings and parts lists.

Examples of the software you might use include AutoCAD and Fashion Studio.

Activity:

Design a CAD system for a retailer to use.

Unlike two-dimensional (2D) graphics packages, CAD programs usually have a set of ready-made 3D shapes that can be used. These shapes are referred to as **objects**. Objects are created by combining simple shapes, often known as **primitives**. Most CAD packages also allow the user to add textures, colours and tones and even add lighting effects.

Once an image has been created, 3D effects are achieved by **plotting** co-ordinates creating a **wire frame image** which is then rendered (covering the wire frame to make it look solid). The rendered image can be rotated and re-sized. CAD packages require a powerful computer processor to perform complex mathematical operations. CAD packages can generate very accurate drawings which can be **reduced** in size or **enlarged** without losing accuracy. Different types of **line** can be used for drawing and images, including **3D** images, can be manipulated on screen. They can be flipped vertically or horizontally, and rotated.

A CAD package has far more standard shapes than a simple drawing package, which can be used as basic tools for drawing. It can also perform **calculations** on designs. For example, it can calculate the actual length of lines from a scale, and work out the areas of the shapes that have been drawn to scale. It can also carry out costings on a design.

Typical applications of a CAD program are:

● in architecture, to produce designs for building

● in traffic control, to produce detailed drawings of road junction layouts

● in engineering drawing of all kinds, for example to produce the exterior and interior designs for cars

● in any other industrial context where accurate drawings are required – for each application, a set of standard library shapes is available, for example electronic components for circuit diagrams

● in fashion design.

Shop design drawings are usually too large for a printer, and are printed using a plotter to output the finished designs.

Obtaining an output

A plotter is a device for producing high quality graphical output on paper. It can produce plans, maps, line diagrams and 3D drawings. Plotters come in sizes that match the standard sizes of paper, and can be very large.

There are two main types of plotter:

● **Pen plotters** use pens to produce images,and different pens may be used, containing different coloured inks. The pens can reach any point on the piece of paper. The lines drawn are continuous, not made of dots, and the drawing produced is very accurate. Pen plotters may be classified as either **flat-bed** plotters, or **drum plotters**. On a flat-bed plotter, the paper is held stationary on a flat surface. On a large flat-bed plotter, the paper may be held in place by suction from underneath.

On a drum plotter, the paper, usually in a roll, is held on a drum that can be rotated backwards and forwards.

● **Penless plotters** use various different technologies. High quality work for publication is produced by electrostatic plotters.

Output is slow from a plotter, but speed is less important than accuracy for the type of graphics it produces. Technical drawings for a kitchen design, for example, must be accurate.

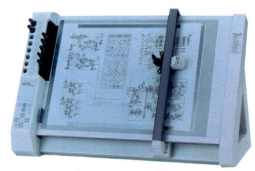

Outputting a design on to a plotter

Electronic point of sale (EPOS) and electronic fund transfer at point of sale (EFTPOS)

This is located at each till and in a supermarket consists of a keyboard, a digital display, a scanner which reads barcodes, a set of scales, a printer, a credit/debit card reader and a till drawer. The difference between EPOS and EFTPOS is simply based on the way the customer pays. If the customer pays with cash or by cheque, EPOS is used. If the customer pays with a debit card, the money is automatically deducted from the customer's bank via the EFTPOS system. Each till has its own base to which all of the above is attached.

This base unit is connected by cable to the branch computer in the supermarket's systems office. The branch computer controls the stock. Data about goods being sold is fed into the terminals, and, as well as providing customers with itemised bills, these systems also generate useful management information.

Stock records are kept up to date automatically and management can monitor which lines are selling well, and which are not so popular. They can observe seasonal variations in buying, and can see whether customers in one area buy different products from those in another area.

It is very rare that in a large supermarket you will find individually priced goods with their own label. Instead, there will be a price on the shelf. In some supermarkets computerised shelf edge labelling enables shops to adjust prices across all branches from a central computer. This system is currently being used by Makro in the UK. This is because the electronic systems which are used widely nowadays need to be as efficient as possible and so each product is given a barcode.

Barcodes in retailing

It is much cheaper for a shop to use barcodes as staff can change the price of goods by altering the price on computer, without having to re-price each individual product. Only the label on the shelf needs alteration. (See above.)

Once the data has been collected from the shopping, the branch computer searches its stock for the matching **EAN number**. When this is found, the computer sends back details of the price and description of the article to the EPOS till.

This information in turn is printed out on to the receipt and adds the price to the total. While all this is taking place, the branch computer is recording how many items have been sold.

This, in theory, removes the need for manual stock-taking as it is already done. In practice, theft and data entry errors cause marked differences between virtual and real stock levels.

Activity:

Explore security and other systems that can prevent stock loss through theft.

Activity:

Explore methods of improving the accuracy of stock level data.

Re-ordering

1. At the end of each day the branch computer sends details of every sale to the main computer at head office.

2. Using the information, the main computer system updates records of the number in stock of every item in the store.

3. Using a forecast of sales along with other factors such as weather and the time of year (for example if it is winter the supermarket may not want to re-order 200 ice lollies as they will not get sold), the system automatically orders the correct amount of stock.

4 The main computer also transmits these orders to computers in the distribution centres (large warehouses storing products ready for delivery to stores) via telephone lines.

5 These distribution centres then send the required stock by road to the stores.

6 Price changes and prices of new products, special offers, etc., are sent back to the branch computer in the supermarket.

7 New shelf labels are printed and the night staff at the supermarket place these on the shelves ready for the following day.

The flow chart below shows the process of re-ordering described above.

Input	Process		Output
Barcode	Decoded		
	Stock file	Product details and price →	Digital display and receipt
	One item deducted from stock		
	Is stock level less than re-order level?	Yes →	Supplier and re-order file
	No ↓		
	Stock file updated		

A supermarket's re-ordering process

There are always two branch computers linked to the EPOS terminals at the checkouts. They record information about items sold and provide backup for one another. If only one computer was used and broke down, the shop could not function properly.

These branch computers are linked via telephone lines to a large main computer. This computer is situated at the shop's head office. All branches of the shop are linked by phone to the main computer.

Monitoring and control

Computers are also used to control freezer and chiller cabinets. Individual sensors inside each cabinet monitor the conditions and switch the motors on and off. Computer control enables a supermarket to store different foods at different temperatures, for example ice-cream at −15°C and fresh meat at 4°C. The head office computer can keep a continuous check on all of the freezers without the need to have a member of staff check temperatures each hour. This reduces the risk of food thawing and being wasted.

Activity:

Explore a range of automated control systems used in a supermarket.

Data on customers

One advantage of the introduction of ICT to supermarkets and shops is the ability to collect data on customer preferences.

While the general data collected offers the retailer valuable information on trends and preferences by store, the information cannot be linked to individual customers. To assign information to individual customers the retailer needs names and addresses plus a method of encouraging each customer to pass on their details each time they shop.

The way most companies encourage customers to provide them with information is to give them something in return.

Internet-based retailers have easy access to purchaser data through cookies and passwords (see pages 101–2). Traditional high street shops have to look for other methods. The form below is used by Tesco to collect data on its customers.

To encourage customers to provide the necessary data, the customer gains points each time he or she uses a Tesco loyalty card. At the same time the company gains valuable information on each purchase the customer makes. Store cards have led to sophisticated databases and enabled shops to know more about their shoppers than they did a few years ago. (In small communities, this used to be true as shopkeepers knew each of their customers personally.) Some advanced retailers know customers' shoe sizes, clothes sizes, favourite colours, whether they have pets, favourite foods, whether they have gardens, etc. This enables the store to market new offers and products directly to customers and to target special offers based on how much each customer spends.

The use of store loyalty cards and customer reference numbers allows for two-way dialogue. Frequent flyer awards have been offered by airlines for some time. Customers collect 'air miles' based upon how far and how often they fly. These are then used for upgrades and free flights. The airline can target specific customers with special offers.

A loyalty card and application form used by Tesco. The form shows what data Tesco wants on its database alongside any shopping information it will keep

Some retailers have taken this approach still further. They look at customers' previous purchases, compare them with the broader population and then target specific offers at customers based upon the data. The more you buy, the better the shop's data on your likes and dislikes and the more data it will have on the likely purchases of people like you. Personalised recommendations are sent to you direct.

Activity:

Explore ways of building customer profiles based upon past purchases.

Online shopping has also led to a growth in the promotion and sale of personal information. Information that retailers gain on customers, such as what they buy, how they pay, and address and credit card details, has become big business. Over 10 000 lists of personal information can be rented at present. Very few people realise how much information is held about them. The Internet is ideal for building audience profiles as it is possible to track every purchase, and even record the things the customer looks at before buying.

Using customers to help run the business

One supermarket chain pays its customers to point out problems such as incorrect freezer temperatures, goods past their sell-by date and product names that have been misspelt. The supermarket is encouraging its customers to act as quality control checkers.

The clothing manufacturer Levi Strauss has found a way to encourage its customers to keep buying Levi's jeans. Customers buying a Levi's Personal Pair™ are measured for a pair of jeans. Their measurements are sent electronically to the factory where their jeans are made to measure to fit perfectly. The online system then records this information for future orders. As long as the customer does not change shape, he or she always has an easy way of ordering personalised clothing. Digitoe is a company making made-to-measure shoes in the same way.

After-sales service

Another area of retailing that is changing as a result of ICT is that of after-sales service. Shops and retailers can use ICT to keep in touch with customers. Some products even include sensors to enable the retailer to monitor their function. The sensors then send the data back to the retailer by mobile or landline communication methods.

This is ideal in products such as cars, refrigerators and washing machines. The retailer can monitor, for example, engine performance, and even tell the customer when his or her car or appliance needs to be serviced.

Coca-Cola is using remote systems to monitor stock levels in drinks vending machines and Otis to monitor the use and performance of lifts in buildings. The monitors check the wear and states of components.

Sensors can even be used to personalise an item to suit the user. Police forces around the world are experimenting with smart guns. The guns are programmed by the retailer with the registered handler's hand details or a special microchip hidden in a bracelet or jacket. Without the link of the correct handprint, the gun will not fire.

Other products are being built so that they can be upgraded using new technology. Software has been sold like this for some time but now there are upgradeable washing machines that can be altered to suit new materials and washing powders.

There are also upgradeable car engines that can be modified to suit driving styles and new fuels, and even upgradeable microwave ovens. You buy the product from the retailer, register your name and address, then buy and download upgrades as they become available. If you want to change the styling you will need to buy a new product, but all other features can be changed.

Activity:

Design an online registration system for purchasers of goods.

Impact of computer systems in retailing on customers, companies, employees and society

Computer systems have considerably changed the way people shop and how shops and supermarkets are run. The advantages of using ICT in retailing do not appear immediately as management has to

invest in new equipment and staff training, and there will always be a changeover period while staff are learning about the new systems.

Some shops have had computer-operated stores for over 15 years. The introduction of ICT has brought benefits to both customers and retailers.

Advantages to customers	Advantages to retailers
Faster checkouts	More efficient stock control
Better itemised receipts	Less chance of checkout staff making mistakes
Fresher goods because stock levels can be lower	Performance of staff can be monitored
Wider selection of goods	Better security
More special offers	Less warehouse space needed
Many different methods of payment	Shelf pricing more cost effective
Chilled and frozen foods kept better – reduced health hazards	Fewer excesses/ shortages of stock
	Better cash flow due to electronic fund transfer
	Easier to predict sales
	Easier to market goods

Benefits of ICT for customers and retailers

By using ICT systems to monitor purchases, large retailers can provide goods to suit the local market. They are able to ensure that the correct sizes, colours and products are available in an individual shop based on past customer preferences in a particular area.

The systems can even forecast future sales based upon past sales at certain times of the year. By linking the system to weather stations, for example, they can forecast sales based upon local weather.

Activity:

Design a local weather tracking system.

Activity:

Design a system that can use past data to forecast future sales.

Being able to forecast future sales also helps retailers to make management decisions such as how many staff are likely to be needed at different times of the day and year.

A negative impact

ICT has enabled the large supermarket chains to expand from small shops that served only about 100 people a week to superstores serving over 11 000 people a week. This development has taken place largely because of the efficiency of computer systems which ensure that the store always has the right levels of stock and the items that customers want to buy.

Traditionally, people would go to the high street or town centre to buy goods in a variety of small specialist shops such as the greengrocer, the grocer, the butcher, the baker. Now superstores stock everything under one roof and because they are able to buy in bulk, they are able to sell at prices that are usually cheaper than in the small high street shops. Superstores are usually located outside the centre of town where there is plenty of space for car parks. While many people like the convenience that they bring, with their long opening hours, not everyone has benefited from the rise of the superstore.

Small businesses in towns have lost a lot of their business to the supermarkets, and many have closed. They cannot compete with supermarket prices, nor opening hours. Superstores are able to stay open for very long hours, sometimes 24 hours a day, because of computerised systems. Smaller shops without such systems would have to employ more people if they wanted to open for longer and keep up with the big stores, but this would be expensive.

Big supermarkets are not always good for small communities that still need to rely on their local shops. For the customer, if you don't have a car and cannot get to a superstore, then you are at a disadvantage.

Changing working practices

The bigger supermarkets have a large number of staff, most of whom work part time. ICT systems are used both to draw up staff rotas and to calculate staff pay. Even though the job of a cashier sounds very tedious, the work does have its benefits.

You need no special qualifications and the training does not take very long. Instead of computers replacing work, they actually provide more work (however, some special skills are needed) because the computers need people to run them, input data, and make sure they are operating properly.

Activity:

Design a staff rota system for a large shop.

Barcodes, in particular, have speeded up checkout procedures and changed the job of a cashier. Before EPOS and EFTPOS were introduced, each item was individually priced (there was no barcode). Instead, the cashier had to add up all the prices on the till. Supermarkets using ICT have been able to change the image of grocery shopping. Large stores have cafés and more checkouts to make everything run as pleasantly as possible.

Another change in working practices brought about by the introduction of ICT is that regular tasks like stock-taking, which used to be very time-consuming, can all be carried out automatically by computer, saving a lot of time and manual labour. The only items that need to be manually counted are the more expensive items like alcohol and specialised foods. Re-ordering stock is also easy to do.

With computerised control of stock-taking, sales and pricing, retail outlets are able to stock a wider variety of products to keep customers satisfied so that they will shop there again. The larger the store, the more people it is able to serve.

TESCO

```
                                          £
WATERCRESS                             1.19
MUSHROOM CLS/C
0.255 kg @    £2.38/ kg                0.61
ORG BCH CARROT                         1.49
GINGER 125G                            0.59
FINEST PEPPERS                         1.39
SPROUTS 500G                           0.95
ORGANIC TOMATO                         1.39
CORIANDER                              0.69
ORGANIC TOMATO                         1.39
BABY POTS LSE
1.085 kg @    £1.79/ kg                1.94
ONION SHALLOTS
0.405 kg @    £2.29/ kg                0.93
ORG AVOCADO                            0.79

TOTAL                                 13.35
VISA DEBIT                            13.35
CHANGE DUE                             0.00
===========================================
CLUBCARD STATEMENT
===========================================
CLUBCARD NUMBER 63400400028947955*
POINTS THIS VISIT                        13
TOTAL UP TO 04/10/01                    279
===========================================
FREE DELIVERY ON EVERYTHING FROM OUR
            WINE WAREHOUSE

Choose from our entire range by the case
 Don't worry if you're not sure, we'll
 help you make the right selection and
       also deliver to your door.
 Visit our New Online WINE WAREHOUSE at
             www.tesco.com
     but hurry, offer ends 13/10/01
-------------------------------------------
         OPEN 24 HOURS

  Monday 08:00 until Saturday 22:00

       Sunday 10:00 - 16:00

           THANK YOU
    FOR SHOPPING AT TESCO
            ABINGDON
      STORE TEL (01235) 707400
   PHARMACY TEL (01235) 550332
GARDEN CENTRE TEL (01235) 707444

 If you have any comments about today's
  shopping trip, please let me know

       DANNY MANSFIELD
      CUSTOMER SERVICE
           MANAGER

6/10/01  17:06  2008  006  1004  9184
```

Receipts contain a lot of information

Computer systems can also control security, heating and lighting in large stores. ICT is used to guard against stealing by staff and customers, control heating and ventilation, and open automatic doors.

Shop items can be tagged so that anyone removing them from the shop without paying will set off an alarm. To achieve this, sensors are placed close to the entry and exit doors. The tags can be removed or inactivated at the checkout when the purchaser pays. CCTV cameras can be used to watch for shoplifters.

Activity:

Design a security system for a shop.

ICT has made a difference to the way superstores attract more business. Data stored on computer can be used to assess the success of different items available for sale, and promotion of new goods can be directed to certain markets using information gained from sales records on customer loyalty/reward cards.

This has enabled superstores to attract more customers by offering more and more varied products from all over the world. For example, in the summer, many of the large supermarkets now provide ready prepared barbecue meats and accessories such as special cutlery. These supermarkets are always trying to emphasise the fact that they provide great quality food. At the same time, it is all prepared and takes about 30 minutes to cook.

For the customers, apart from everything being quicker, more efficient and having a wider choice of food, computer systems can be used for money-off, or multibuy schemes.

If they did not have efficient computerised systems, supermarkets would not be able to offer multibuy schemes (such as buy two and get the third free). The barcode of the item which is to have a saving is entered into all the computers and every time it comes up, 50 per cent, or whatever the reduction or offer is, automatically goes through and comes out on the receipt.

Activity:

Design a system suitable for multibuy purchases.

Use of computerised systems means that it is easier for management to monitor the work of staff, behaviour of customers and supply of foods and other consumables. All staff records can be kept on computer, staff appraisals can be recorded on computer and even recruitment can be carried out via a company website.

Activity:

Design a payment system for staff wages based upon hours worked.

Global marketing

The Internet allows retailers to sell their goods to a world audience.

Taxation has become a major problem in Internet sales. Internet shopping is a free-for-all, with few regulations. One tax affected in the UK is VAT (value added tax). When goods are purchased outside the European Union, VAT is paid only on goods that cost more than £18.

This means it is cheaper to buy two CDs separately than together. Prices of goods vary all over the world. Timberland shoes, for example, are half the price in the USA than they are in the UK. This makes purchases considerably cheaper outside Europe. There is also a problem in who collects the tax on a purchase that originates outside the European Union.

At present, Consignia (the Post Office) or a courier company acts as an agent to collect duty and collects it through either the delivery person or Consignia. This system could not cope with increasing Internet sales.

Another big issue on taxation is if someone orders an MP3 music file (the replacement for CDs), or a piece of software and downloads it over the Internet, there is no mechanism for levying taxes or import duties, and at present, the purchaser avoids paying any tax whatsoever.

Censorship

In the late 1980s the Internet was opened up to the public and became a communications phenomenon. Nobody could predict the speed with which people all over the world would start to use this new form of communication. In 1995, there were an estimated 56 million Internet users worldwide; by 1999, this figure was 200 million. A wealth of information is readily available to those who possess the technological means to access and contribute to it. However, some individuals and governments are worried about this availability and have introduced censorship of Internet communications.

Today, in many countries, governments have imposed restrictions on the Internet in an attempt to limit the presence within their borders of information that they classify as offensive or threatening. Different governments try to restrict access in different ways, using regulation and outright bans. However, obstacles to free speech on the Internet do not end there; control of the development of the Internet industry by large companies also creates obstacles, as do regional inequalities in terms of access to the new technology, since many parts of the world still have little or no access to the Internet. Taken together, some people believe that these obstacles serve as a giant barrier to the free flow of information and the ability of individuals to profit from the enormous potential of the Internet as a medium of interactive and democratic communication.

It is easy to argue in favour of control over the contents of particular websites, for example those related to child pornography or exploitation. The exercise of control itself, however, gives some people power over what others should or should not be allowed to see. Those who exercise power will always have their own views and beliefs.

Perhaps the most obvious form of Internet censorship is the sweeping measures that governments use to control not just availability of information on the Internet but also the ability of its citizens to participate in the global exchanges that take place online. Many types of measures have been introduced by authorities, particularly in several authoritarian regimes.

In some countries, the security services actively patrol cyberspace and keep track of Internet users in the country. They can block access to a number of sites and areas on the Internet that they believe offer material unsuitable for their citizens or that are not in agreement with government views.

Another way that governments use to control the Internet is to try to regulate internet service providers in terms of what they are allowed to display. Since the Internet was not specifically designed with security in mind, communication on the Internet is rather like sending online postcards that anyone can read, or pictures that anyone can look at. The only way to secure data being sent is to use encryption (see pages 96–8). A number of governments, however, will not allow encryption unless their security services have ability to read the encoded messages.

This has led to a number of individuals attempting to take governments to court as they say that any restriction on private Internet communication is contrary to the protection of privacy written into a number of international treaties/ documents; for example, Article 12 of the Universal Declaration of Human Rights and Article 17 of the International Covenant on Civil and Political Rights.

The ability of governments and companies to view personal communications over the Internet has led to the introduction in the UK of the Regulation of Investigatory Powers Act (2000). This Act regulates the interception and observation of individuals' Internet communications. Its main purpose is to ensure that the relevant investigatory powers are used in accordance with human rights. These powers cover:

- the interception of communications
- the acquisition of communications data (for example, billing data)
- intrusive surveillance (on residential premises/in private vehicles)
- covert (hidden) surveillance in the course of specific operations
- the use of covert human intelligence sources (agents, informants, undercover officers)
- access to encrypted data.

For each of these powers, the Act will ensure that the law clearly covers:

- the purposes for which they may be used
- which authorities can use the powers
- who should authorise each use of the power
- the use that can be made of the material gained
- the use of independent legal opinion where necessary
- a means of redress for the individual.

Where large companies dominate Internet activity, they are a powerful influence on communications. Large companies can publicise their points of view by spending huge amounts of money on Internet services, and this can push out smaller companies, with less money to spend, that might wish to express alternative views. Some people believe that the computer giant Microsoft has a virtual monopoly in computer operating systems and the software market, and that this affects free speech as well as the variety of information available. Could Microsoft or any other large organisation really control all information in the future? What would be the effects on free and open communication on the Internet?

These questions need to be asked when there is a real danger that one person or organisation could have such complete control over power and information in the so-called Age of Information.

● The future

Society has generated a different target audience, cash rich and time poor.

Information and communication technology has changed the way we buy our goods and services. With longer working hours and less leisure time, weekend shopping has become a chore for many shoppers. Electronic shopping could take care of regular, repeat grocery shopping but real shops need to build upon their social functions.

Fear of crime has also encouraged some people to stay inside their secure homes and cut themselves off from the outside world. The shop could become a centre of the community again, becoming a therapeutic place. The worst scenario is that the high income, technologically literate sections of society will live in walled cities of secure, high-tech zones from which they will electronically order all their requirements while keeping the lower-income information-poor communities out. The future could be a more impersonal world that disadvantages large sections of society such as the old, frail and poor.

Designing information systems

A GCSE student using a computer system

To satisfy exam requirements, you will need to design your own information system, using commonly available software, and this section will help you to do this.

● What is an information system?

A computer system is perhaps the most obvious example of an **information system**. The various devices that make up the system are called **hardware**.

The computer itself may be a desktop, laptop, notebook, palmtop or personal digital assistant (PDA).

The size of computers is being reduced all the time. For example, small programmable devices that are called computers are fitted inside cars and can control the operation of the car, as well as carrying out other tasks such as direction finding. These have replaced the dedicated microchips that used to perform a similar, but more limited function. Many modern-day devices are controlled by microprocessors although it is not always obvious that they are.

A standard computer system that would be used in an office or school or at home consists of a number of components or parts – the computer itself, and other hardware devices that are connected to it. These hardware devices are referred to as peripherals. Details of peripherals that allow input of data and those that provide output of information are illustrated throughout this book.

The hardware typically supplied with a computer system includes the computer itself (containing one or more hard disk drives), a screen, a keyboard, a mouse and one or more additional disk and CD drives. The system can be shown in a simple diagram like the one opposite.

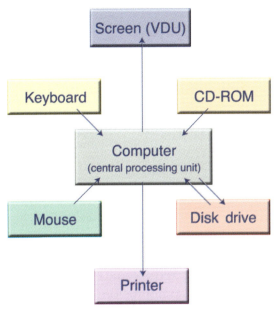

A computer system

When you are designing your own systems, you should try to illustrate them like this. Notice the way the diagram uses arrows to indicate whether the components of the system relate to input or output.

The largest computers are mainframe computers. These are used in situations where vast amounts of processing power and data storage ability are required. Banks, large insurance companies and utility companies such as suppliers of electricity and gas use mainframe computers. These very powerful machines produce considerable amounts of heat, so mainframe computer rooms have to be air-conditioned. Some mainframes are water-cooled.

Your system will not be based on mainframe computers, but you will be able to simulate the same types of data processing and design a functioning system.

Systems life cycles – development of systems and sub-systems

The systems life cycle is the series of development stages that any information system goes through. These are:

- **analysis** – finding out what is needed

- **design** – producing detailed designs for all the parts of the new system

- **implementation** – actually producing the new system by setting everything up on the computer

- **testing** – making sure that the new system works as well as it should

- **documentation** – producing guidance about how the system works, or how to use it, for the people who will have contact with it

- **evaluation** – checking how well the system performs all the tasks it was designed to carry out.

Designing a system to satisfy exam requirements

To satisfy exam requirements, you will need to design your own system following the above stages. The first step is to choose and describe how and where your system will be used. This consists of deciding what data should be input into the system, and what output the system should produce.

You will need to produce evidence to prove that you have worked your way through the design of a systems life cycle. This evidence will take the form of notes, diagrams and screen dumps.

An important early step is getting to know as much as you can about the potential user(s) of your system and what their needs are. It is worth spending some time examining the benefits and drawbacks of the existing system before you attempt to design a new one. There is no point in having an ICT system that is less effective than the existing system, whether it uses ICT or not.

You will need to contrast and compare alternative ways of achieving the desired outcome. This should include both ICT and non-ICT solutions.

Due to restrictions of equipment and software, your system may not truly reflect the types of hardware and software that would be used in a commercial setting. If this is the case, you should explain the differences between the system you are using and a commercial system.

Inputting data

You will need to consider how the data can be entered with both accuracy and speed. This will involve considering the needs of the user for whom you are designing the system, and how data errors could occur. For example, a system used in a hospital could be operated by busy nurses. Restricting the amount of information displayed and the options available could make your system easier to operate and thus reduce possible errors.

Inputs

Once the type of input has been established, the type and method of capturing the data needs to be considered. Inputs may consist of:

- numerical data
- pictures
- sounds
- text
- movement.

The frequency and volume of input needs careful consideration before the input device can be selected.

System output

You will need to consider the types of information the user of your system is likely to want as an output of the system. This involves describing different types of outputs and the benefits and drawbacks of each for the system you have designed.

Outputs can take many forms and may include:

- an invoice, receipt or bill
- a dispatch note
- a packing slip
- a screen display
- a sound.

Again, before the system can be designed it is important that the type of output is considered. Frequency and volume of the output must also be taken into account.

Selecting hardware and software

In designing the best solution, you will need to consider a range of hardware and software. You should make sure that you compare and contrast the alternatives. No single answer will be perfect for any given circumstance. You need to find the best answer for your chosen context.

Choosing the right software for the job

One of the most important aspects of system design is ensuring that you use the right software.

In designing your own systems you will need to draw up a specification before choosing the right software for any given situation. The following checklist can help you to do this:

1. Plan a framework for an evaluation report (normally on a word processor). Each stage of the evaluation can then be described in an organised way in this report.

2. Scan read or watch the software documentation (publicity material/ manuals/tutorials if available) to see whether:

   - the program can be used to produce the outcome that you hope for

   - the package is easy to use – does it tell you clearly what to do? Is it easy to look up things you need to find out? Are good examples provided?

3. Think of some suitable test data that can be used to run the program. Enter the data and try out all important aspects of the program.

4. Make sure the program is user friendly:

   - Are the messages clear?

   - When data has to be entered, is it easy to understand what is required?

   - Does the software sometimes make you wait an unreasonably long time, or without explanation?

   - Is the entering process simple with this software? (For example, does it make you do more keying than necessary?)

   - Can you get the program to do what you want?

5. Check that the methods of input and output suit what you want to do and the type of data you have.

6. If the program is interactive, is the type of user interface suitable?

7. Find out if the program is versatile and adaptable. Can it cope with a variety of situations? If your desired outcome changes, will the software be able to cope?

8. Check the program is reliable. This means that it should do what the manual says it does. Does it carry out all the tasks required as described in its manual?

9. Check the program is robust. This means that it can cope with errors in data while it is running. Try to make the program go wrong. Enter incorrect data for each response. A good program will validate all data before processing it. If the data does not make sense, the program should find this out and request that you re-enter it.

143

Designing information systems

Applications packages, including integrated software

You will probably be using a standard applications package, but there are other types of software available.

An applications package is an item of software that has been designed to perform a specific function in terms of outcome, or for use within one particular industry. Examples of specific functions are word processing, spreadsheet creation and management, or database creation and management.

Integrated software consists of a matching collection of applications packages that are designed to be bought and used as a set. An integrated package is likely to include software for word processing, spreadsheets, databases and graphics and may offer other features also. Integrated software is normally less expensive to buy. Commands are normally common throughout the package, which makes them more user friendly. Moving data from one program to another within the integrated package is normally simpler than between separate packages.

A disadvantage of integrated packages is that they may be very strong in one particular area, such as spreadsheets, but relatively weak in another, such as graphics. If a user wants one particular function that is going to be used a lot, it is better to find a separate, specialised package.

Tailor-made software

Where there is a particular requirement, a company may employ its own experts to write in-house software, or it may employ a software house to write specialised software on its behalf. Such software is very expensive and is used only in companies with large computer departments, or where no suitable ready-written applications packages are available. An example of this situation is the traffic control department of a county council. The department looks after the flow of traffic throughout the principal town in the county. At each road junction controlled by traffic lights there is a control box that controls all of the traffic lights and any pedestrian crossings at the junction. The heart of the control box is a tiny computer chip that contains all the information necessary to keep traffic flowing smoothly through the junction. The program for each chip is individually written at the traffic control office to meet the characteristics and requirements of the particular junction. No two junctions are the same.

If you model a traffic system, you will not be able to use the type of tailor-made software that is used in a real situation. Your system will rely upon standard control software packages and readily available sensors.

General purpose packages

A lot of ready-written applications software is not specific to a particular type of business. Some database packages, for example, can be used to develop tailor-made software. General purpose packages are very popular because their documentation (manuals, tutorials, etc.) is usually excellent, programs are well tested, and they are inexpensive.

General purpose software is sometimes called **content free software**.

Although you will use standard software, the processing that the system has to do must be designed. Processes may include searching, sorting, performing calculations or producing text or graphics. If the solution is based on an existing package such as a spreadsheet or database package, it will be possible to produce simple descriptions of what must be done and the software will do most of the work. The description of what must be done is known as an **algorithm**.

Where a suitable package is not already available, it will be necessary to write a more detailed algorithm to explain how the program will work.

An algorithm is a sequence of instructions that tell how to solve a particular problem. An algorithm must be specified exactly, so that there can be no doubt about what to do next, and it must have a set number of steps. A computer program is an algorithm written in a language that a computer can understand. The same algorithm can be written in different languages.

There are various ways of describing algorithms, including flow charts, structure diagrams and **pseudocode**. Pseudocode is an outline of a computer program written in a mixture of programming language and English. It is one of the best ways of planning a computer program.

● System design

To help you work through an effective design process, let's examine how professionals would design a system. You will not have to follow all of these steps, but your portfolio will have to demonstrate your knowledge of the design process.

There are a number of different ways that professionals design systems, but the following steps demonstrate a typical design sequence.

Analysis

This is where you use interview, research and investigation to find out what a potential user would want and what is already in place. You may wish to use the Internet, text, questionnaires or talk to people to gain this information. You will need to compare alternative solutions and examine issues such as ease of use and appropriateness.

To get the best performance from an information system, it is very important to be clear about what the system must do. Many systems have been unsuccessful because no one has really worked out what is needed. **System analysis** is the process of finding out exactly what the system must do.

You will need to show that you have a good understanding of what your system must do.

In many ways, analysis is the most important stage because all future developments are based upon it and changes may be difficult to make later on. Usually, a computer system is developed to replace an existing manual system, or a more primitive computer system. A good starting point for analysis is therefore to examine the existing system – how it works, what improvements are needed, and what future developments may need to be considered.

You can use a number of methods to examine an existing system:

● Observe it being used. See what happens to data entering the system and what types of output there are. Effective observation takes time. It shows the conditions under which the system is used, and may draw attention to points that users of the system might not mention themselves.

● Interview people who use the system, at all levels. Ask them what they think is good or bad about the system.

● Questionnaires can be useful where a lot of people use a system. However, it is important to think carefully about the kind of questions to ask. Be aware that people may feel threatened by the introduction of a new system. Questionnaires give people time to think about what they want to say, and they may be more willing to criticise a system in writing than they would be in front of others.

● Describe the existing system. A diagram is often useful to show the flow of data through a system.

At this stage, a professional would produce a **feasibility report**. This would explain whether a new system would be better than the existing system, and would give reasons. It would outline what could be achieved with the new system.

The following details are likely to be included at this stage:

● Objectives of the proposed system.

● Facts about the parts of the old system that are being replaced by the new.

● Any constraints on the system, that is limitations on solutions to problems. A constraint might be the amount of space, or finance, available.

● An update of cost-benefit analysis based on the new information.

Where a system is being developed from scratch to suit a new requirement, it will not be possible to learn from an existing system. It will be necessary to discuss and analyse carefully the requirements of the new system and build on these.

The analysis sometimes leads to a feasibility report which asks questions like 'Is it worth doing?' and 'Will it work?' As long as the feasibility report recommends that a new system will be an improvement on the old one, further analysis will be carried out to determine exactly what the new system has to be able to do.

A **requirement specification** is then usually produced. It will detail all of the inputs that will have to be produced, and all special user requirements also. As it is unlikely in a real commercial situation for only one person to be designing a system, responsibilities of members of the team involved with the project will be set out, with deadlines by which stages must be completed.

Although you are probably working on your own, it is worth drawing up a schedule or timetable to plan when you will complete each stage of your coursework.

The requirement specification will form the basis for later stages in developing the system and must therefore be detailed. The people using the existing system must be able to understand it, and it must be checked with users to make sure that the new system will do everything that is required.

It must also be checked to ensure that there are no conflicts in the list of requirements. For example, a user may want a system to be developed using a particular database package, with ability to store and manipulate pictures. If the package will not allow the manipulation of pictures, it means that the requirements conflict.

Users can be unrealistic about what can be achieved in a new system and the requirement specification must ensure that all hardware and software proposed is capable of performing the tasks required.

The requirement specification can be used later to check that the new system is being put together properly, and it can be used as the basis for evaluation of the completed system.

Design, implementation and testing

Design

Designers of large systems first break down the system into sub-systems.

Designers will need to break a design problem into a number of sub-tasks and then design a system to carry out these tasks. Your coursework will probably focus on only one of these sub-systems. Implementing and testing is an important part of design. You should constantly review your solution and modify and refine it as you go along.

Remember to consider carefully the input and output of your system alongside methods of checking accuracy. The system must now be designed to meet the requirement specification.

It is often useful to break down a large system into sub-systems that are easier to work with. For example, a supermarket information system might be divided into the following:

- Customer section. Scanning of items purchased, production of customer receipts, taking care of customer store card information.

- Banking section. Accepting payment from customers and corresponding with banks to obtain direct payment when debit cards are used, and payment when credit cards or cheques are used. Updating store and central accounts.

- Stock control. Monitoring information about stock moving in and out of the store. Ordering stock whenever needed. Providing information about levels of sales.

A structure diagram can be produced to show how the sub-systems fit together to make the whole system.

In the design stage, it is very important to think about the way each part of the system interacts with its users. This **human user interface** should be consistent throughout the system. The following points might be considered:

- Use of colour. Colour can be useful to highlight messages, but too many colours can be confusing. There should always be good contrast between colours so that words are readable and images clear. Red is often considered to be a warning colour, so might be kept for warning messages. The designer must bear in mind that some users may be colour blind so it will be best to avoid combining red and green or blue and yellow.

- Sound. Sound should be used only where it is essential. Music systems require sound, of course, but it would be a distraction in an accounts system. Warning sounds can be used, and sound may be useful in certain situations, for example, barcode readers in supermarkets normally bleep to indicate correct reading.

- Flashing symbols. These can be used to attract user attention, but the designer must be aware that certain flash rates can cause epileptic fits, and flashing symbols can be distracting and annoying.

- Location of items on the screen. The designer will try to keep the same items in the same place on all screens forming part of the system. This will make the system easier to use. Users tend to look mostly at the top third of a screen and important messages like error messages may not be seen if they are placed at the bottom of a screen.

- Movement from screen to screen. The designer should make sure that the same method is always used to move between screens. It is irritating for users if some screens need just a key-press when others need a specific word, followed by the enter key.

- Making choices. The designer should also make sure that the same method is always used where users have to indicate that they have made a choice. The input device used is likely to be the mouse or the keyboard, but should not be a mixture of the two as this makes the system much harder to learn.

- Appropriate use of language. The designer will make sure that the type of language used is suitable for the users of the system. Graphics may work better than words in some cases.

Implementation

During this stage, the hardware and software that have been selected are installed in their working positions, and set to produce the required outputs. It is common for a large new system to be implemented in stages, with the most important sections being installed first.

As each section is implemented, it will be tested thoroughly and when the entire new system is complete, a full system test will be carried out.

It would be very unlikely that a hospital, for example, would want to suddenly replace the existing system with a new one before ensuring that the new system would work effectively.

There are three common ways of installing systems in organisations:

- **Direct implementation**. This method is normally used only where a small system is being implemented. All of the users begin to use the system on a certain date. The method is quick and simple where no problems occur. It is not so suitable for larger systems because, despite testing, problems do often occur in the early stages of implementation and if all users tried to switch at the same time, there could be chaos.

- **Phased implementation**. This method introduces each task separately and ensures that it is running smoothly before another task is brought into the system. For example, in a supermarket, the stock control section might be implemented first. Disadvantages are that implementation takes much longer, and benefits of the new system are delayed.

- **Parallel running**. In this method the new system is started and run alongside the old system, which can act as a back-up if problems develop with the new system. Results from the new system can be compared with results from the old system. However, since each job is carried out twice, there is more work for users and each job will take twice as long.

Testing

It is important that a new system is thoroughly tested before it is introduced. Test data to be used in this process will have been devised during the design stage and testing is carried out regularly throughout implementation of a system. The general principle of testing is to check that the system works properly with typical data, data at the limits of what is allowed (extreme data) and data that is wrong. It is also necessary to check that the system meets all of the requirements set out in the requirements specification, and that it will be acceptable to the users.

The testing of the system can be broken down into five stages:

1. The system is tested with data that contains no errors to see if it produces the correct results.

2. The system is tested with data that contains errors to see how this data will be processed. Ideally, all the errors will be picked up by validation procedures but it is impossible for the computer to detect every type of error.

3. The system is tested with very large volumes of data to see if it can handle this, and if it might be able to cope with increased work in future.

4. System processes that are required only occasionally are tested. An example might be the production of a salary report on a certain day of the month.

5. Extreme data is entered into the system to test how this is processed. The range checks included in the validation program should detect any unsuitable data.

If the results of all tests are positive, the system can be introduced, or implemented.

Documentation

The final stage is to produce user documentation. This should address both technical and normal users. You will need to test your documentation to ensure its effectiveness and modify it as a result of these tests.

Documentation of a system is very important and is likely to be divided into two distinct types:

- People who use the system every day will need clear instructions to get the best results from it, but they do not really need to know how the system works. They will need **user documentation**.

- People responsible for maintaining and repairing the system do need to know how the system works, and may have to adapt the system as user needs change. They need **technical documentation**.

User documentation

This will take the form of a user guide or manual that users can turn to when they need to learn new procedures, or deal with problems that arise. The guide should cover points such as how to load the software, how to perform everyday functions, how to save and how to print.

The various jobs that the system can do should be described in a logical order. Illustrations may be used to help explanations, and the guide may include examples and exercises to help users become familiar with the new system. It should have a contents page and an index to help users find the answers to their questions, and a glossary that explains any new terms may be useful.

The guide should tell users what to do in exceptional circumstances. For example, if data is sent to a printer when the printer is not switched on, the user will need to know what steps to follow. However, the user guide will not provide technical details that are not needed for everyday use of the system.

Technical documentation

This will explain the system to the programmers and systems analysts who will be responsible for maintaining and possibly adapting it. The documentation will be written in precise technical language and will include test data and the results of testing. In the longer term, it may be invaluable to explain the working of the system to a new expert who was not around when the system was implemented. Like the user documentation, technical documentation also requires a contents page and index.

Evaluation, applications and effects

Once you have designed and built your system, you should explore the benefits and drawbacks of the system you have designed for the people who will use it. You will also need to check and justify any

benefits your system brings over other methods used. You should identify any training needs that result from the introduction of your system.

A full evaluation of a new system is carried out when it is all installed and running.

The evaluation will be based on criteria set by looking at the requirement specification that was produced at the end of the analysis stage. A full evaluation will demand detailed answers to a range of questions designed to determine whether the system carries out all required tasks properly, and how well it achieves each task. A scoring system may be useful in a full evaluation, and it may indicate areas where changes will be needed.

As the system and its users settle into regular use, evaluation sessions are likely to be carried out at regular intervals. Users of the system will always be consulted in such evaluations as they are the people who will be aware of any problems. Present constraints such as time, money or numbers of qualified staff may be looked at with a view to making improvements in future.

Describing the benefits of using ICT, and any drawbacks

Your coursework should contain a critical look at the use of ICT in the chosen context. You may wish to consider changes in working practices, changes in job profiles, and system performance. You will need to demonstrate that your own thinking has been modified as a result of your investigations.

System flow charts

System designers use flow charts to represent their systems. By using flow charts, designers can graphically show how a system works. **A system flow chart shows in general terms the operations that will be performed on information in an information system.** All a designer has to do is to consider all the stages that operators and equipment will go through when the system is used. Each stage is then represented using these standard symbols. Many more symbols are used on a system flow chart than on a normal flow chart.

These are the symbols that may be used in system flowcharts:

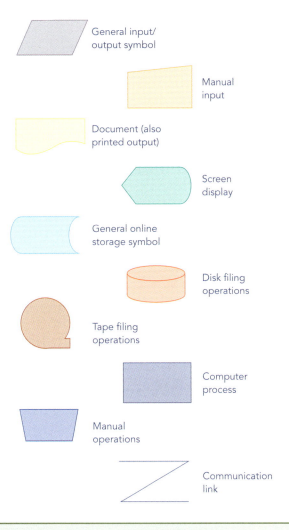

General input/output symbol

Manual input

Document (also printed output)

Screen display

General online storage symbol

Disk filing operations

Tape filing operations

Computer process

Manual operations

Communication link

As an example of a system flow chart we will explore a ticket-issuing system for a theatre. The designer does not have to use a separate symbol for each and every action that the theatre does. For example, if the operator makes some text bold, adds some pictures and adds word art, these will not be shown as separate activities. Whilst these are all computer processes, building a process flow chart for all these activities would be a waste of time. The designer does have to show the main operations of the system.

The theatre box office assistant answers the telephone and welcomes the caller. The assistant may tell the customer first about opening times, etc. These are all manual operations that do not involve the computer in any way. So the first symbol in the flow chart would be:

Answer phone
Talk to customer

The next stage is to load up the booking package on to the computer (a disk operation).

Load program

Output will be on screen.

Booking system
Output to screen

Then we move on to input the text (a keyboard operation) and automatic checking of credit card and booking availability and printing of tickets.

By now you should understand which symbols should be used for each of these operations.

Of course the system we have described here is simple and linear. In practice the theatre's system will be far more complex. In a real theatre booking system all of the following actions need to be represented.

Hardware

- the theatre's box office desktop computer is used to communicate with the main computer at the theatre's central booking centre.

Software

- records of existing customers are maintained using a database program
- data is validated as it is entered
- records are automatically updated as tickets are booked
- a communications program is used to connect the computer to the main booking centre.

Data capture

- part of the data comes from the main computer centre
- part of the data is provided by the customer, in writing through registration forms, or via the telephone to the theatre's booking office.

Data validation

- data forms and addresses are checked for accuracy by theatre booking staff
- data is validated by the computer on entry.

Files

- the main data file for each customer includes a range of typical fields.

Updating

- at the start of the year, people who have not booked tickets are copied to another file and after a number of years deleted from the main file
- new customers are added
- small changes are added by office staff during the year.

Other processing

- statistics are calculated on ticket sales for various shows
- varieties of lists are produced for administrative purposes.

Output

- tickets are printed
- lists are printed
- screen booking systems are constantly updated.

Index

153

Index